CW00411077

For Philippa

The Author at Camp 14

ARKA TAGH

The Mysterious Mountains

William Holgate

 **THE ERNEST PRESS**

Published by The Ernest Press 1994
© William Holgate

British Library Cataloguing-in-Publication Data
A catalogue record for this book is available
from the British Library.

ISBN 0 948153 33 4

Maps drawn by the author. Photographs were taken by the author &
Tim Martin.
Acknowledgement is made to the Royal Geographical Society for
permission to reproduce the photograph of Saint George Littledale.

Typeset by EMS Phototypesetting, Berwick upon Tweed
Printed by Kyodo Printing Co.

Contents

Acknowledgements

My greatest thanks go to Tim Martin for his (largely) uncomplaining support and companionship.

I would also like to express my gratitude to Graham C. Greene for his wide-ranging efforts on our behalf and to Baring Brothers and the British Academy for their generous financial assistance. Finally, I would like to take this opportunity to acknowledge the no less indispensible help and encouragement of the following:–

Shirin Akiner, Hassim Adje, Francis Baring, Professor K. Brannigan, Nick Clinch, Jeremy Cantwell, Nick Crane, Chen Xi Fei, Chinese Academy of Sciences, David Clark, Nick Danziger, Embassy of the Peoples Republic of China, Jane Enticott, Great Britain – China Centre, Anders Hojmark, David Hughes, Huang Min Min, Dominique Hemard, Nelly Hermitant, Charles Holmes, H. E. Ji Chaozhu, Abdullah Kanje, Neil Lindsey, Li Dan Hui, Helen Lai, Liu Kui Yu, Lu Min, Michelle Lewis, Peter Molnar, David Mathew, Professor K. Murta, Nicola MacBean, D. I. Marshall, Patricia Martin, Peter Norris, John Pilkington, Tony Payne, Jill Payne, Bill Rowe, Royal Geographical Society, Dave Rothery, Stephanie Smith, Mark Salter, Sheffield University, Sino-British Arka Tagh Association, Dean Smith, Philip Snow, Twenty Seven Foundation, Teng Tingkang, John Town, Wu Mei, Phil Wilson, Wang Hai, Wang Da Wei, Chris Warby, Nicolas Wolfers, Jane Woods, Tusan Yakup, Ying Chin, Zhou Shifu, Zhao Yen.

CHAPTER 1

White Patch on the Map

The first threads of snow came spinning in the wind, caking each camel's topknot as they passed. Hassim's doleful song tailed away, his hunched figure pitching back and forth as we loped across the valley floor. Far to the south the last pools of pallid sunlight fled up whitened ramparts to meet a thickening sky. We were now two days out from Bash Malghun and three hundred miles of desolate plateau and ice-clad mountain stretched ahead before we would once again enjoy its doubtful comforts. But even the sputtering farts of Hassim's flatulent camel couldn't dampen our mounting excitement as the Arka Tagh came at last within our reach.

The fateful choice of the Arka Tagh had taken place over ten years before in the midst of the Pennine winter of 1980 – but from the deceiving security which comes from lounging in front of a blazing log fire while the snow falls benevolently outside. Looking for a new challenge after years of inactivity, I had basked in the fire's glow and scanned map after map until my attention was caught by a white patch adrift in the dusty brown wash of Central Asia. Here were the Arka Tagh, intriguing and to me unknown – but even more intriguing was their sheer isolation. Straddling the border of Xinjiang (formerly Chinese Turkestan) and Tibet they were surrounded by formidable natural barriers, each sufficient challenge in its own right. The arid wastes of the Taklamakan Desert to the north were mirrored on the south by the desolation of the Chang Tang or Tibetan Plateau. To the east stretched the salt plains and swamps of the Tsaidam whilst the intertwined ranges of the Kun Lun provided impressive defences on the west.

It's tempting to put the choice down to serendipity but I'm sure

1

there were several more or less conscious influences at work. I had been drawn to wild places since my first childhood hikes on the Yorkshire Moors and this fascination had grown over the years into the love of mountain exploration which was now the source of my search. But there was also a streak of perversity in my nature which made me shy away from classic areas such as the Himalaya and look instead for a less travelled range. The isolation of the Arka Tagh suggested they would qualify under this heading at least.

I was drawn too by the books of Eric Shipton, one of this century's greatest explorer-mountaineers. Shipton had been British Consul-General in the great Silk Road oasis of Kashgar in the 1940s and one of the few people to circumvent the prohibition on climbing in Xinjiang, although not, as far as I knew in the Arka Tagh. But even at base in Kashgar he conveyed, as no other, the compelling magnetism of the region;

> Each morning I woke with a sense of wonder that I was there in the very heart of Central Asia, in a dream world of mountains and deserts and measureless distance

Was the distance still measureless I wondered, or had it been circumscribed by the intervening years?

There was one final and, in retrospect, ironic factor in my search – I was looking for somewhere that wouldn't need a large party or years of complex organisation. My enjoyment of the mountains came not from conquering unclimbed summits but rather from scrambling slopes more suited to my limited abilities. This meant that large expeditions were unnecessary and in the past I had often found a party of one quite sufficient – and my enjoyment all the more keen as a result. But even as I chose the Arka Tagh I had a dawning suspicion that they might exact a compromise on this point.

For the time being, it was an irresistible prospect and I set about learning more.

My first approach to the Mount Everest Foundation set the tone for the next five years, the Secretary, Brigadier Barker-Wyatt, replying that the range had been "excluded from the areas to which the Chinese authorities were prepared to allow access for expeditions". At this stage I still didn't really see myself as an expedition, but it seemed a minor point. The Brigadier referred me to the Chinese Mountaineering Association in Beijing for further information. In fact, all my approaches including those to the Chinese Embassy ended up sooner or later at the door of the Chinese Mountaineering Association in Beijing. Unfortunately, the CMA, in what I came to recognise as a traditional Chinese response, simply didn't reply. And there the matter rested as each new angle was greeted with the same inscrutable silence.

The first half of the eighties wasn't totally wasted, however. Whilst my attempts to get into the area were frustrated, the search for information proved marginally more fruitful. By ransacking the hallowed alcoves of the Royal Geographical Society whenever I was in London and the no less hallowed (by the owners) shelves of second-hand bookshops when I wasn't, I slowly managed to gather a sparse collection of references to the range. It must be said that the harvest was hard won and fairly meagre at that.

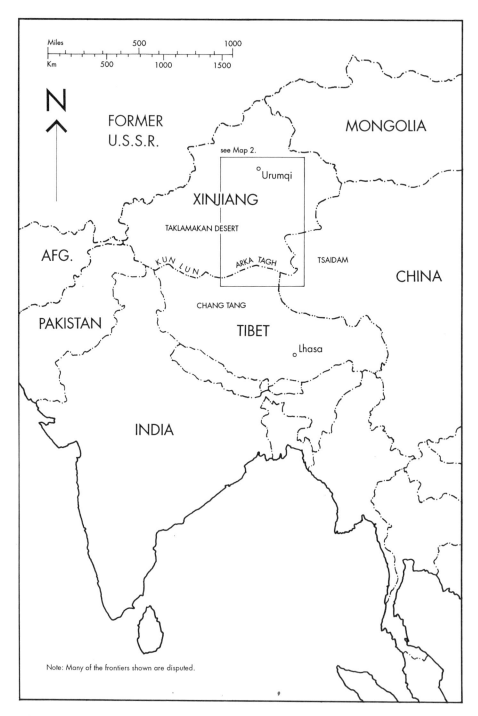

Map 1. Location

CHAPTER 2

The Mysterious Mountains

By far the most productive sources of information were the
chronicles of western explorers, particularly those from the closing
years of the nineteenth century. During this period there was a great
upsurge in the exploration of Tibet and Xinjiang by Europeans and
in many cases their accounts remain the best available today. Yet
although there was an expansion of interest in the region, this
tended to concentrate on two specific areas. The first was the
complex knot of mountains at the junction of the Hindu Kush,
Pamir and Karakorum where players in the "Great Game" crossed
back and forth in a seemingly continuous caravan of international
intrigue. The second was Lhasa, capital of Tibet, which was the
elusive goal of one western explorer after another. This "Race for
the Holy City", as it has been called, was in fact a race for
nineteenth place, as Lhasa had already been visited over the
previous four centuries by a Dutchman, Van de Putte, an English-
man, Manning, and at least sixteen assorted Catholic missionaries.
Its lure, however, seemed undiminished, as indeed it does today.

The Arka Tagh, lying over 500 miles from both areas, were
generally neglected except when they were encountered by those
few explorers foolish or brave enough to approach Lhasa from the
north. This was no mean ambition as it entailed either crossing or
circumnavigating the Taklamakan Desert before attempting chain
after chain of uninhabited mountains with the Arka Tagh at their
core. The lack of settlements introduced a further complication as,
unlike much of the Himalaya, neither local produce nor porters
were available and provisions for the whole journey had to be
carried by pack animal. In turn there was little grazing and further

5

animals had to be engaged to carry fodder for the first animals. And so on. True, there was game, but this rarely provided more than a minor supplement to the expeditions' supplies.

The first European to investigate the northern approaches was the great Russian explorer, Nikolai Przhevalsky, best known today for his discovery of the wild Przhevalsky's horse. Przhevalsky started a decade of exploration by men (and one woman) of unusual character. In the words of his biographer, Donald Rayfield,

> A man of ruthless determination and of shy tenderness, an apostle of European superiority who loathed European society, an explorer of China who despised the Chinese, a big-game hunter on an epic scale who mourned the death of his dogs, a major-general who disliked the army, a materialist and a Byronic Romantic, he had the paradoxical temperament and universality of genius.

It was Przhevalsky's consuming dream to penetrate to the heart of Tibet and enter the gates of Lhasa, but although he led four expeditions and made three major attempts on the Holy City from the north-east, his dream was to remain unfulfilled.

By the winter of 1884-5, he had already turned back from his final attempt and fought off a sustained attack by Ngolok tribesmen, helped in no small measure by the inclusion in his party of a Cossack escort. His route now lay homeward but he couldn't resist one last examination of the Tibetan borderland.

Leaving a winter base at the Gas Nor lake he led his men first west up a majestic sweeping valley which he named Dolina Vetrov, Valley of the Winds, and then south between the Columbus and Mosco Mountains. Here, his animals weakening rapidly, he turned back, but not before he had dimly located a further range of high snowy mountains a hundred miles to the south. As they were only indistinct he named them Zagadochny, variously translated as Conjectural or Mysterious, but on his return the Imperial Geographical Society named them after Przhevalsky himself. The name didn't last and Arka Tagh, the Turki name used by the Xinjiang Uighurs, was generally adopted by subsequent travellers. This is often translated as The Far Mountains, but a more accurate rendering would the The Mountains Behind or, with only a sliver of translator's licence, The Hindermost Mountains.

This was to be Przhevalsky's last expedition. He died on the banks of the Issyk Kul in 1888 whilst preparing a fifth journey. Five years later the nearby town of Karakol was renamed Przhevalsk in his honour and this time the name did survive – but few can doubt that Przhevalsky would prefer the wild Equus przewalskii as his lasting memorial.

Przhevalsky was succeeded in 1889 by a French expedition under Gabriel Bonvalot. The party also included Prince Henry of Orleans, whose father, the Duc de Chartres, had funded the enterprise, and Father Dedeken, a Belgian priest who spoke fluent Chinese. Approaching the Arka Tagh from the north, they crossed the frozen Kum Kol Darya (Darya meaning River), receiving an early warning of what lay ahead.

13 December 1889
We see upon the banks the skeletons of camels which have been gnawed bare by the wolves. A little further on we find emerging from the ice the almost intact humps of camels, and upon closer examination we see that part of a caravan has been drowned here, including the camel-driver one of whose arms is raised as if in an attitude of menace or of entreaty.

This passage was to be only too memorable on our own expedition over a century later.

Leaving the Kum Kol Darya, Bonvalot's caravan followed an ancient pilgrims' route over the eastern extremity of the range. As they climbed, virtually everyone in the party was stricken by nausea, breathlessness and headaches, symptoms of mountain sickness caused by the lack of oxygen at high altitude. Whilst the others slowly recovered, the continuing decline of Niaz, one of the camel men, can be followed on Bonvalot's map – Plaine de la Misericorde being shortly succeeded by Passe de Requiem.

Burying the unfortunate Niaz in a shallow grave near the summit of the pass, they fought their way down the southern slopes, thus becoming the first Europeans to cross the range. They pressed on towards Lhasa but were to be denied the ultimate prize, being turned aside three months later by a large Tibetan force less than a hundred miles short of the Holy City.

The expedition's achievement in crossing the Chang Tang in mid-winter was nonetheless outstanding, so outstanding in fact that some British critics at first refused to believe Bonvalot's account, and later scorned the journey as "a haphazard dash, a wild gallop, a flight through the country of a rather pretentious and startling character". As the expedition differed little from contemporary British activities, the comments were more a reflection on the pompous and chauvinistic establishment of the time than on Bonvalot and his intrepid companions.

Although Przhevalsky was dead, his fifth expedition had pressed ahead and in 1890 the new leader, Captain Mikhail Vasilovich Pevtsov, tried an approach southwards from Charchan (called Qiemo by the Chinese), an oasis in the Taklamakan Desert. Like Przhevalsky before him, Pevtsov was eventually forced back, but even as he retreated Jules Dutreuil de Rhins and Fernand Grenard were being appointed by the French Governmnent to undertake a journey of exploration which would include the first European crossing of the central Arka Tagh. First they spent two years ransacking the Kun Lun and Karakorum to the south of Khotan, Dutreuil de Rhins eventually becoming unable to walk or ride and being carried on a litter. He retired to Khotan for the winter of 1892 taking a "short-term wife" in the local custom. In Grenard's words,

> the general sympathy with which he was surrounded restored Dutreuil de Rhins' health, consoled him for his vexations and made him ready once more to tempt fortune.

The two explorers set out from Charchan for Lhasa in the following summer and on 28th September 1893 they finally surmounted the Kara Muran Davan or Black Water Pass and looked

Dutreuil de Rhins

down on the plateau of Tibet. This is not the last we will hear of
them.

To date the score ran France 2, Russia 0, but a third player now
entered the game. Saint George Littledale, a country gentleman
from Bracknell, set out in November 1894 together with his wife and
his nephew, William Fletcher. The party was completed by Tanny,
the Littledales' fox terrier. The Littledales were already seasoned
explorers of Central Asia and this was their third expedition.
Thirty-seven years later, in Littledale's obituary, Sir Francis
Younghusband wrote,

> Mr Littledale was an explorer of an unusual type. He was endowed
> with a sufficiency of this world's goods and... when he travelled he
> travelled for the sheer love of travelling and of shooting new animals.
> Perhaps the fact that he took his wife with him on all his three great
> journeys predisposed people to think they could not have been very
> adventurous or arduous. But Mrs Littledale was no ordinary
> woman. She was of the toughest fibre.

Littledale certainly intended to make use of his ample means. In his
own words,

> My scheme was to strain every nerve to reach Tibet and, if possible,
> Lhasa, with plenty of food and animals to carry it. Most of the other
> expeditions had failed owing to their arriving in a more or less
> destitute condition and then, of course, the Tibetans could dictate
> their own terms. We also relied upon bribery and went well pre-
> pared with the sinews of war for wholesale corruption.

After travelling via Constantinople and Samarkand, the Littledales were faced with crossing the Tian Shan between Russia and
China in the depths of winter. However, in an example of the wary
international freemasonary which existed between the explorers of
Central Asia, their route had been provisioned in advance by
Colonel Grombchefsky, "the stormy petrel of Russian frontier
advance" and they crossed the Terek Pass "without any material
discomfort".

They arrived in Kashgar on 5 January 1895, where they en-

Saint George Littledale

countered the Swedish explorer Sven Hedin, who was yet to make his most famous journeys. True to his promise, Littledale spared no effort in provisioning and fitting out the expedition and it wasn't until 12 April that the party finally left Charchan for Lhasa, their initial route closely following that of Grenard and Dutreuil de Rhins. Littledale's story, like that of Dutreuil de Rhins, will appear many times in the coming pages.

While Littledale was fighting his way over the Arka Tagh, Hedin was engaged in a life or death struggle of his own. Having set out to cross the Taklamakan from west to east, he had run out of water and already two of his men were dead. Hedin himself survived only by crawling on hands and knees to a pool in the bed of the Khotan Darya. The experience did nothing to quench his thirst for exploration – the next year he set out to cross Tibet from west to east. Littledale had described him as adding "considerably to the merriment of the party" but like Przhevalsky, Hedin was to dedicate his life to the exploration of Central Asia, and the decades of hardship which this entailed were to give him a reputation for toughness, determination and not a little arrogance. Commenting some years later on Sir Aurel Stein's turning back from another difficult desert crossing, he wrote,

> I should never have made such a decision. I should have continued through the desert. It might have been the death of me and my men. I might have lost everything, as in 1895. But the adventure, the conquest of an unknown country, the struggle against the impossible, all have a fascination which draws me with irresistible force.

Hedin's 1896 route joined those of Dutreuil de Rhins and Littledale shortly before the Kara Muran Davan. Here a large body of his men made off north with both money and provisions but were soon caught and returned to camp. Hedin had the ringleader brought before him and held a summary court by moonlight, pronouncing sentence of a dozen strokes of the rod.

After crossing the Kara Muran Davan, his route led off east, the journey passing with, for Hedin, relatively little incident although all but seven of his fifty-six animals had died by the time he reached the Tsaidam.

Four years later he returned, crossing and recrossing the range further east and, in the process losing Aldat, his Afghan guide, to mountain sickness. Finally, he made a determined attempt on Lhasa but received the same rebuff as those before him, his departure towards Ladak marking the end, for the time being, of western activity in the range.

Hedin himself continued to return to Central Asia, pitting himself against both nature and bureaucracy for a further thirty years. He lived on until 1952 but his authoritarian and increasingly right-wing attitudes combined with his growing disdain for British achievements, resulted in his backing the losing side in two world wars – and by the time of his death he had long been deprived of the recognition he craved.

Sir Francis Younghusband's entry into Lhasa from the south in 1904 effectively removed the spur to further attempts from the north, but the critical factor in the European withdrawal was essentially political as successive administrations in both Xinjiang and Beijing took an increasingly strong line against exploration by westerners. A silk curtain descended on the Arka Tagh and it would be almost a century before Europeans returned to the range.

Of course Europeans weren't the only travellers to enter the area, but my researches had inevitably centred on their works as I could find no accounts by Uighurs, Chinese or Tibetans. There were certainly many early chronicles of journeys along the Silk Road through Charchan, of which the best known is probably that by Hsuan Tsang in the seventh century. But in all these accounts, the Arka Tagh remained unremarked, hundreds of miles to the south, hidden behind the intermediate ranges. In contrast, those few native hunters, gold prospectors and pilgrims who did see the range over the centuries left no written record. From time to time they, or their relics, appear in the western narratives, but their own stories remain untold. One of Littledale's men, a Ladaki named Ghulam Rassul Galwan, later wrote of the journey in his book *Servant of Sahibs*, but this resolutely sycophantic volume is, unhappily, the closest we come to a native account of the mountains.

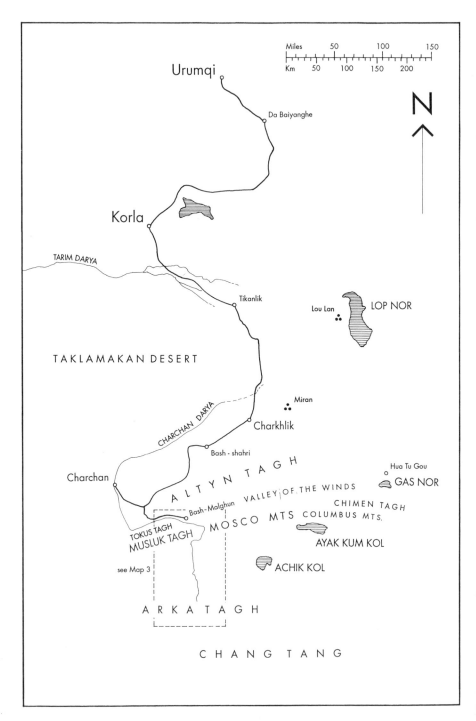

Map 2. The Approach

CHAPTER 3

Arrest

By 1986, the well of historical research was running dry but my official approaches to the Chinese were no further forward. I was frustrated at every turn. Drastic measures were needed – if I couldn't get into the area officially then I'd try it unofficially!

Unfortunately up-to-date intelligence on approach routes was proving even more elusive than historical information. Despairing of squeezing anything useful out of the Chinese I was reduced to quizzing modern day western travellers. The main problem was that anyone who had been to Tibet was automatically assumed to have plumbed the furthest recesses of the country. Time and again I made contact with someone who had "crossed the Arka Tagh" only to find on closer investigation that he or she had driven along the main Golmud – Lhasa highway hundreds of miles to the east. It was clear that the opening of previously forbidden areas was very selective. Most of Tibet and Xinjiang was still off-limits to independent travellers.

Then, at last, the curtain twitched. I learned that a joint Chinese-American expedition had climbed Ulugh Mustagh, the highest mountain of the range, in the previous year, 1985. It turned out that leaders Nick Clinch and Bob Bates had been applying to the CMA for permission since 1973. The Chinese had finally relented and agreed to a joint Chinese-American expedition to commemorate the 30th anniversary of Xinjiang's (latest) incorporation into China, an event the Americans might otherwise have omitted to celebrate. The fact remained that with a seven-year lead, an impressive climbing record and the patronage of George Bush, they had succeeded where, so far, I had failed.

The expedition itself seems to have been rather a trial for the Americans. The Chinese had already established an approach route over the Achik Kol Plain the previous year, and the party, which by now had expanded to fifty-four members, was driven to the base of the mountain in twelve army trucks. Five Chinese eventually reached the summit and two were later rescued by the Americans after falling on the return. One does not need to read between the lines to detect a certain Sino-American tension.

It seemed that Eric Shipton had, after all, known of the range. Bob Bates, who had climbed with him in 1966 reported him saying of Ulugh Mustagh,

> It's probably the hardest place in the world to get to, harder than the Antarctic because the land around is so high and nobody lives near it. Bill Tilman and I had hoped to get there but it is too far in.

Shipton himself, in *Mountains of Tartary*, appears to refer to a completely different Mustagh to the south of Khotan, but I assume both he and Bates knew the difference between the two.

I had no plans to climb the peak itself but at last I had some useful information on approach routes. The area didn't seem to have lost its ability to impress, Nich Clinch describing it as "about as bleak a place as you can imagine". It was still uninhabited but obviously less inaccessible than before, given official permission and the right transport. However, although the eastern approaches had been opened up, the area to the north and west of Ulugh Mustagh remained, as far as the Americans knew, largely unexplored.

Meanwhile, having omitted to provide myself with the patronage of George Bush, I still didn't rate a reply from the CMA. In a desultory effort to circumvent this, I wrote to the other Chinese institutions involved in the American expedition, suggesting that they provide logistical support for a two-man British team (and implicitly obtain permission on our behalf). It was a long shot and I didn't really expect a response so, once the letters were sent, I promptly forgot about them and returned to the unofficial approach. I advertised:–

China. Attempt to reach Ulugh Mustagh. Very unofficial trek. Initiative needed. Success doubtful. Apply to Box...

Even this was too much for the editor of *High* magazine who insisted on cutting out "Very" as he said it made the trip sound illegal. So true.

Fifteen people replied, including one who obviously took the "initiative" part seriously. He spent two pages listing different ways he could kill people – his arsenal ranging from Carl Gustav anti-tank weapons to credit cards. The clincher came when I noticed that "married" had been masked out of his curriculum vitae and replaced by "widowed". As the prospect of laying waste the Chinese population didn't appeal, I sent details to the other fourteen.

My plan was to travel as ordinary tourists and try to bluff our way into the "closed" area. Once there, we would try to find pack animals and head off towards the mountains. On hearing the details of this scheme – and to their everlasting credit – Chris Warby and Phil Wilson were the only two of the original fourteen who still wanted to go. Chris was a tall, stooping, gangly youth in his early twenties – fifteen years younger than me – and rarely varied from the quiet, rather diffident manner he had at our first meeting. He put me in mind of a hesitant stork. Phil on the other hand was an extrovert and couldn't bear to be still for a second. Much the same age as Chris he had short spiky hair and talked in high-pitched staccato bursts. At the side of Chris's stork, he was a restless cockatoo with a machine gun.

It was obvious that one of our main problems would be navigation as we still couldn't find any decent maps of the area. General maps of Tibet and Xinjiang were consistent only in their mutual contradiction, one in the Times Atlas even showing a rather unconvincing road over the Kara Muran Davan itself. As for the immediate approaches of the Arka Tagh, the best available maps were still the route surveys of de Rhins, Littledale and Hedin from a century before. But these covered only thin corridors along their routes and would be little use elsewhere. In the end, we decided to use satellite photos. Technically these are images built up from a continuous scan of reflectance values – but the resulting products are very similar to photographs and, with some allowance for distortion, can be treated as such. I managed to borrow three negatives from a friendly university but we had to buy a fourth from NASA. We had them blown up to a metre square each, the limit of resolution, which gave a scale of 1:250,000 or about four miles to the inch – fine for touring through Europe by car but still ridiculously small scale for the purpose in hand.

Our preparations were already well advanced when, to my amazement, one of my fishing letters had a bite. Huang Min Min of the Xinjiang branch of the Chinese Academy of Sciences replied that my proposal was "very interesting" and suggested a joint expedition. After the deafening silence of the previous seven years this should have been the signal for unbridled celebration – but Huang's timing was atrocious. As the joint expedition sounded like it would be very big, very expensive and require years of organisation, we decided to press ahead unofficially.

My only previous journey to China had been a truly red carpet affair and the 1987 journey was to act as a stiff antidote. It began well – we breezed through Beijing customs, our NASA maps, ropes and dehydrated food happily undiscovered, and flew on to Urumqi, the capital of Xinjiang, without a hitch. But from here on we had to fight our way onto a succession of dusty trains already crowded to overflowing by a kaleidoscope of Central Asian nationalities and their livestock. First we headed south, the most direct route, until turned back by the police at Korla. Then we started on a long sweep east and south to approach the Arka Tagh from the Tsaidam.

It was on this leg that we were introduced to the fragile relationship between the local Uighurs and the Han Chinese. As we pulled out of one mountain halt, a young Uighur bystander started smashing the train windows with large hunks of coal. His target, a detachment of Chinese soldiers further down our carriage, poked their rifles through the holes but didn't fire.

Leaving the railway at Liuyuan, we turned to buses, following desert roads first to Dunhuang and then to Da Tsaidam and Golmud in Qinghai Province. Here we were again halted, our onward route via Urt Moron and Tart proving to be totally devoid of traffic. Discouraged, we retraced our steps to Da Tsaidam where perseverance paid off and we finally managed to bluff our way into the closed area.

Our bluff relied on nothing more than the locals' confusion over the prohibition, encouraged by our own evident confidence in our right to be there. But it seemed to work and for the next four days we ploughed steadily westward, the settlements, mainly oil camps, gradually thinning as the desert intensified. The roads bore no relation to those on our maps but we were even more startled to find one guide describe the area as "the lush grasslands of Qinghai". Eventually we reached a small town called Hua Tu Gou beside the Gas Nor lake.

Hua Tu Gou itself was hell on earth. Pigs rooted amongst rubbish tips, mounds of excrement and treacly pools of crude oil, the whole capped by its own orange-grey cloud of pollution. Yet it was situated in the midst of stunningly beautiful scenery. To the north and east the Akato Tagh rose dusty and brown beyond a wide plain, whilst to the south and west the snow-clad Chimen Tagh formed a vast wall behind the Gas Nor. Lying in a hollow at the centre of the plain the lake glistened in the sun, deep blue with a white salty margin. As I looked across its gently rippling surface my years of research came alive at last.

Both Przhevalsky and Hedin had established bases at the lake but the only British parties to come near had been Carey and Dalgleish who had passed to the west in 1886 and Peter Fleming who had celebrated his twenty-eighth birthday with Ella Maillart thirty miles to the south almost half a century later. More recently, two Americans, Douglas Mackiernan and Frank Bessac had rested here in 1950 whilst fleeing the communists. Both Dalgleish and Mackiernan were later murdered, providing a grisly continuity of sorts.

Unfortunately, Hua Tu Gou was to mark the limit of our own progress. We had already made contact with some Mongols from

Alaer, a nearby settlement, and built up hopes of hiring horses when we were discovered by the police, and put under house arrest. This was later relaxed as far as the town boundary whilst they tried to ring regional headquarters for instructions. Luckily the lines were down but this only postponed execution and after an initial fruitless attempt to win them round we bought three bicycles in the town shop with the intention of skipping bail. Not surprisingly our plan was soon discovered and, after a tense confrontation we were summarily deported from the province.

It was a release after a fashion as we hadn't been the most compatible of travellers and we split up to go our separate ways. My own route led first to Lhasa and then to Kashgar, both of which more than fulfilled the promise built up over the preceding years. Finally, all that remained was to return home and take up the official approach again.

With this in mind, before leaving China I travelled back to Urumqi and, much to his consternation, dropped in on Huang Min Min. I found him in a corner of the Academy campus, a dusty collection of concrete buildings on the northern outskirts of the city. He was about forty and had a round face with deep set eyes which disappeared completely as he gave me a wary smile. He was a geographer and proudly presented me with a paper on glacial run-off he had published in the west. I didn't think it necessary to mention my recent activities and we concentrated instead on the outlines of a future expedition. Huang confirmed that much of the area of the north-west to Ulugh Mustagh was still unexplored. As I had suspected, the road confidently shown crossing the Kara Muran Davan in the Times Atlas was in fact pure fiction, faithfully reproduced by generations of remote cartographers since the time of Dutreuil de Rhins and Grenard. Huang suggested that September would give us the best chance of entering the area, as the rivers would by then have subsided from the spate of summer meltwater, yet the worst of the winter blizzards would be still to come.

He clearly offered the best chance of obtaining official permission so I suggested we should be Joint Leaders, a proposal that obviously appealed. We agreed to keep in touch, parting with the first of many pledges of undying friendship between our Two Great Peoples – a state of affairs that was to prove sadly elusive in our personal dealings.

1988 lay fallow, largely from my own inertia, but further aided by Huang's lapsing into the traditional silence in response to my letters. Two notable advances came towards the end of the year. The first was the introduction of Tim Martin as a potential fellow traveller. He was suggested by Jeremy Cantwell, a mutual friend who helped us selflessly for three years but resisted all invitations to join the expedition itself. As Jeremy knew us better than most it may have been simple self preservation. We were also joined by Neil Lindsey who had been on a recent expedition to Bhutan with Doug Scott.

Our collaboration didn't start off too well, the new year opening with both Tim and Neil in hospital, Tim was a punctured lung and Neil with a slipped disc. Both recovered but Neil later pulled out for personal reasons. Tim stayed and became an invaluable partner.

I had found Phil impossibly garrulous in 1987 and Tim was engagingly phlegmatic by contrast. Put the other way, Phil had found me impossibly laconic and Tim proved better able to cope with this aspect of my character, if indeed it exists. Tall, heavy and with a shock of prematurely grey hair, he was also disturbingly suave, but this didn't seem to impair his underlying abilities. I had wondered, on first meeting, whether he had been softened by too many years of expense account living, but reasoned that a few weeks in Xinjiang would soon cure any tendency towards luxury. Like myself, Tim had long experience of solo scrambling and he had also done some recent climbing on rock and ice. However, neither of us had previous experience of organising an official expedition which, with all other avenues blocked, was the road we would now have to follow.

Tim brought the average age of the expedition members up to forty, but we were still spring chickens compared to most of our nineteenth century predecessors, or even the Americans (average

age 52). Of course, most of them had been considerably younger
when they had first conceived the notion of climbing the range, the
average period of gestation between conception and arrival being
about ten years. On this reckoning I still had two years to go.

The second major advance came when Graham C. Greene,
Chairman of the Great Britain-China Centre, heard of our plans
and offered his help. He later became our Patron, proving every bit
as potent as George Bush. His support was particularly crucial in
convincing potential sponsors of our bona-fides and in lending the
weight of the British Establishment to our dealings with the
Academy. Status (if only borrowed) is an essential ingredient for
success in China.

I had already put a revised proposal to Huang for a joint
expedition and this was eventually accepted in principle, subject to
agreement on expenses. The Chinese insisted on advance negotiations in Urumqi so in May 1989 I flew over via Beijing, passing
student demonstrations in Tien An Men Square en route. The
whole trip entailed six days' flying bracketing four days of solid
negotiations.

My descriptive powers are frankly unequal to the task of explaining how Byzantine and essentially dire this process is. Our
discussions followed no system of logic recognisable as such in the
west, the Chinese taking an enthusiastic delight in exhausting every
last nook and cranny of a given subject before announcing that it
was, in any case, irrelevant to the matter in hand. Alternatively on
the rare occasions when a conclusion did seem imminent new and
unrelated factors were sure to be introduced, thus completely
destroying progress to date. My response was to pursue what I
imagined to be a "polite but firm" approach (although Tim would
later describe it as "gladiatorial") and keep in mind Grenard's
dictum;

> Impatience in Asia is the most serious and the most dangerous of
> faults.

But alarm bells were already ringing as the Academy staff

displayed a surprising lack of knowledge about conditions in the south of the province and even less about organising an expedition. So they looked to me to do calculations of transport and supplies and then demanded outrageous prices to provide them. Luckily we had already reconciled ourselves to the mark up, regarding it as a form of subsidy to the Academy but I often had to draw a limit to our largesse, particularly as we hadn't yet raised a penny to meet it.

These negotiations were typical of many over the coming years and to save repetition and boredom the reader will simply have to take on trust that all official discussions both now and later lasted an eternity and were built on the solid foundation of mutual incomprehension between our Two Great Peoples. The agreement concluded on this occasion can safely be ignored as it was immediately overtaken by events, in this case the Tien An Men massacre. Contact with Urumqi was broken yet again.

Silence reigned until early the following year, 1990, when Huang resurfaced and a new agreement was made. Under this, we would travel south from Charchan, substantially following the routes of Dutreuil de Rhins and Littledale as far as the Arka Tagh and return over the easier Achik Kol Plain to the east. The team would have two British and two Chinese members and would use camels as only the eastern section of the route was accessible by truck. Huang was to be leader of the Chinese members and two Uighur camel drivers and I was to lead Tim. Tim graciously acquiesced,

> "At base we are all tools of your ambition, William, and delighted to be so."

By now, the Chinese expenses had been beaten down to less than a third of the original demand but we had still made little progress in raising any funds to meet them. The joy of the mountains buttered few parsnips with most commercial sponsors, our main targets, and we soon found ourselves searching desperately for a hook on which to land financial support. The character of the expedition and ourselves changed with each new approach. At various times we became wacky eccentrics, sober academics, ambassadors for Sino-British friendship, science or commerce, pioneering explorers, veteran mountaineers or simply guileless amateurs. All had a kernel of truth and we aimed to fulfil our promise under every heading but it was a wearing process – and one we obviously hadn't mastered. We approached a rapidly lengthening list of potential sponsors with dispiriting results. Ian Maxwell claimed, rather prematurely in the light of subsequent events, that the funds of Maxwell Communications Corporation were "quite simply exhausted", whilst Bovis "mindful of the turbulent times in which we live" directed their attention elsewhere. Worried that we were giving the wrong signals, I coloured up our publicity photos so that the army truck behind Huang Min Min looked less like a veteran of Tien An Men. But there was no immediate influx of sponsors and appeals in magazines and newspapers proved equally unproductive.

In desperation we briefly considered making a film documentary but the companies we approached were scandalised at the suggestion that they should pay towards overall costs. The general attitude seemed to be that the film would be such a valuable encouragement to sponsors that a further contribution from the production company was unnecessary. One particularly constipated producer wrote; "It is extremely unlikely that any broadcaster would regard expedition funding as a legitimate use of their (sic) licence fees or advertising revenue."

And so it proved.

As winter snows gave way to spring storms, we came close to abandoning the whole crazy scheme. As many times before, I drifted from the confident assurance that all obstacles would sooner or later be overcome into a morose conviction that my efforts over the last decade had been for nothing. Then, in the depths of our gloom, the clouds parted and a shaft of sunlight lit the road ahead. At the second time of asking, Francis Baring of Baring Brothers Bank, decided we might after all be worth supporting. Tim dealt with negotiations – admirably as it turned out, the first tentative enquiry eventually being converted into a firm commitment. I secretly suspected that Barings had been easier work than the Chinese. Their contribuion, slightly over a third of the total cost, effectively tipped the balance. Somewhere, under the layers of accumulated caution, I was quietly exultant – we would definitely go ahead.

Eric Shipton often boasted that he and H. W. Tilman could organise a Himalayan expedition in half an hour on the back of an envelope, an approach I constantly strove to emulate on our lesser undertakings – and one which had been the model for the (admittedly abortive) 1987 attempt. Unfortunately, our 1990 envelope had necessarily grown to accommodate political and financial factors, considerations which even Shipton couldn't always avoid, but at long last we were dealing with matters for which an envelope should properly be used.

Tim collected equipment, a task complicated by Huang's once again lapsing into silence, whilst I put together a first-aid kit and read up on likely ailments. "High Altitude Pulmonary Oedema" ran the UIAA Guide, "Fine crackles are heard in the chest, and may be audible without a stethoscope..."

I realised with a shock that I appeared to be suffering from High Altitude Pulmonary Oedema at sea level, a fact which might rather complicate later diagnosis in the field. My doctor didn't seem too worried, so I pressed on.

Amongst our other preparations, we managed to fit in a crash course in Turki and a night's camping on the Yorkshire Moors. Together with my smattering of Mandarin, we hoped the Turki would both show willing and, at the same time, give a minimal independence of official translators. As for the camp, it served to prove that Tim and I could stand each other's company for one night at least. By now we were again becoming worried by the lack of response from Urumqi and assisted by our friends at court enlisted the support of the Chinese Ambassador, Ji Chaozhu. I met him to explain our problems and from now on both he and his staff proved a great help, ringing China at all hours of the day and night on our behalf. The result was a telex from Urumqi sending permission for our visas, although it was still notably silent in response to our other requests for information.

Our departure was finally set for 15 August and as it approached, the auguries looked good. The British Academy wrote to say I had been awarded the Stein-Arnold Exploration Grant and we also received a generous private donation. Suddenly at the eleventh hour all the pieces of the jigsaw seemed to be coming together.

Three days before our flight, we congregated at Tim's house for last-minute preparation and packing. We had still received no reply from China to all our queries but sure enough, on the second morning in London a telex arrived, forwarded from my home in Yorkshire. I am tempted to put this telex down to a tremendously subtle sense of humour on the Chinese side. After three years' preparation and with less than 48 hours before our departure, Huang proposed a different route and an expanded team. In addition, we were asked to bring "2 micro telescope, 2 have many function compass, 2 micro memory record, one micro short wave radio" and a pile of other equipment including seven camel bags. Finally, we were at last given an account into which we were asked to cable half the Chinese expenses.

Struggling valiantly to appreciate the joke, we decided to live with the route and personnel changes, ignore the equipment list and cable the money – which arrived after we did.

Preparations complete, Tim took me on one side, away from our respective girlfriends, and had me witness his will.

CHAPTER 4

Breakdown in the Taklamakan

Our arrival in Hong Kong airport again confirmed my theory that to pass through customs the most useful attributes are a crew cut and a mound of khaki kitbags, at least one of which contains controlled drugs. There was even a hint of a salute as we were ushered through without inspection.

We approached the Victoria Hotel with some trepidation until the desk clerk confirmed that Barings were taking care of the bill. It was a great relief given the hotel's pretensions and the bill's likely size. Later we took the tram up to the Peak and had lunch surveying the most tremendous panorama, the sunlit hillsides beside us plunging down to an ever changing forest of skyscrapers and a harbour dotted with toy boats. Beyond, the New Territories and China were lost in the haze. Then, following a jet-lagged siesta we crossed the harbour by the Star Ferry for fresh fried prawns in a Dai Pai Dong or market café, surrounded by the humid evening bustle of the Kowloon streets.

Early the next morning we met David Matthew of Barings and embarked on a day of radio and TV interviews. We had been asked to provide visual aids for the ATV "Morning Life Wave" programme and, loth to unpack the kitbags, had taken our glacier glasses and Petzl head torches. Tim reeled off a reasonably convincing description of snow blindness for the glasses but I shuddered inwardly as he launched into a highly coloured but totally fictitious account of our intention to use the torches to guide our camels by night over precipitous passes. The interviewer was translating our replies directly to camera and we were later told that in the Cantonese version the camels wore the torches.

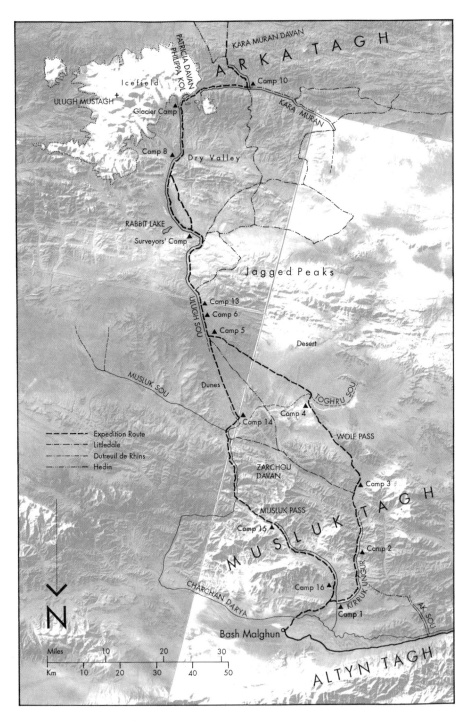

Map 3. The Expedition Route

In the afternoon we had a Press Conference at Barings. This went well, although Tim later swore that I had referred to "finding a chink in their armour" when explaining how I had obtained Chinese permission and we did rather crack towards the end when he was asked what would happen if he were seriously injured.

"I assume Mr Holgate or our Chinese colleagues would go for help," was his reply.

"Ah, but what would happen if you were all injured?" came the inevitable chaser, to which we could only suggest sending a camel with a note. At this point David Matthew thought it best to call a halt.

Having had no previous experience of sponsorship we had been rather apprehensive over just what it would entail and it must be said that David made the whole process thoroughly painless and even enjoyable. That evening he invited us to his flat for dinner.

The flat was in a modern block on the Mid Levels and had a splendid view of the harbour, but its most startling feature was a large Afghan rug incorporating the twin motifs of anti-tank rockets and Kalashnokovs. David too presented a rather startling appearance, sporting an oriental scalp disease and a pair of gold monogrammed slippers. I couldn't decide which I found most disconcerting. He was an old China Hand and before Barings had worked on the mainland for Jardines, acting as liaison for several mountaineering expeditions. His story of one veteran leader going "bonkers" on the mountain was a great revelation. But David's connections with China went even further back and he had a photo of his father meeting Zhou Enlai on prominent display.

"Wonderful for terrorising Chinese bureaucrats," he commented, referring presumably to both Zhou Enlai and the photo.

Later having established that both David and Tim had been to minor public schools I left them to swap memories of fagging and beating whilst I ransacked David's excellent library of books on Central Asia.

Our flight to Beijing the next morning was enlivened by our first taste of fame.

"Hey, you're those famous explorers I saw on TV last night," exclaimed our neighbour. We sheepishly pointed out that we might be famous but we hadn't actually explored anything yet. Our embarrassment was compounded on arrival when we received copies of the Hong Kong papers faxed on by David Mathew. It was hard to recognise either ourselves or the expedition in these fanciful accounts, herds of wild llamas and 9,500 mile high peaks being two of the more plausible obstacles we were expected to overcome. However, as Barings were mentioned in every article David professed himself perfectly satisfied, suggesting the rest was irrelevant detail.

Once settled in, my diary records with relief that Tim was "still fairly easy to get on with – even if his phlegmatism occasionally slips into somnolence". In fact jet-lag seemed to be catching both of us and we slept for most of our two-day stay, rising only for a visit to the Forbidden City.

I had already been enthralled by the City as a visiting architectural student sixteen years before and I still found it impressive. But it impresses not, as most other imperial monuments, by a single burst of splendour, rather by a mounting sense of awe as the visitor is led through each succeeding arch and each enclosing courtyard towards the dragon throne at the centre. In this way the architecture of the City is a revealing key to Chinese society, both Confucian and Communist, for it is the hierarchy of the empire which is glorified, not the emperor himself.

On 20 August we embarked on our final flight – over the Gobi Desert to Urumqi. We were met at the airport by Huang and Chen Xi Fei, a clean-cut young geologist who was to act as interpreter. Chen later announced he wanted a western name for the duration so we dubbed him George and, in order to avoid confusion, he will be George from now on. He had an infectious chipmunk smile which, we came to recognise, accurately reflected the man within and as we jolted our way to the Academy of Sciences campus he brought a light touch where everyone else was conscious of countless unanswered questions. But these were left until the following morning and Huang and George dropped us at the Academy's guest house.

The guest house, like most other campus buildings, was grey, dusty and in serious need of repair. It had some permanent residents but was largely used for "honoured guests", its spartan accommodation representing pampered luxury by local standards. For example George, at 27, was still sharing a dormitory. The guest house effectively segregated us from the local population, or rather the campus population since this was again an elite within the wider city. Our segregation was maintained at dinner when we were ushered into a screened-off section of the dining room. It was one of the perks and the penalties of travelling officially in China. At the other end of the spectrum was a scrum for food in a roadside hovel which I had suffered, and enjoyed, in 1987.

The next morning we met Huang and George to try to pull the expedition together. They were desperate to find out if we had received the last telex, mainly because of the route change. George said government permission had been refused to return by the comparatively easy Achik Kol Plain. No reason had been given but we were presented with a wealth of alternative theories. We were dumbfounded when Huang said he had seen a UFO and footprints of a Yeti on the first expedition in 1984 and he thought the area might have been closed to investigate the phenomena. George preferred to link the closure to the government suppression of a gold rush further east near the Tsaidam. Not to be outdone my own favourite theory suggested the recently reported nuclear bomb test at Lop Nor as the culprit. Maybe the Achik Kol was downwind, albeit four hundred miles away.

"Nuclear? Bomb? Test? Never heard of it," said Huang.

Whatever the reason for the change it left our main objectives unscathed, and we concentrated instead on turning it to our advantage and securing Huang's agreement to try a new pass beside the Ulugh Mustagh ice-field. This looked from our hazy satellite photos as if it would offer a more direct route to the Kara Muran Davan than either Dutreuil de Rhins' or Littledale's routes.

"Interesting," said Tim pointing to the new pass.

"Means dangerous, I think," said George anxiously and so was born the first catch phrase of the expedition. Large snarling dogs were invariably described as "interesting".

We also outlined a completely new route, touching on that of Pevtsov, for the return. Huang was so relieved that we had accepted the change with good grace that he readily agreed to our proposals, subject of course to government approval and always assuming it was possible on the ground.

This meeting provided our first sight of the Chinese maps, Huang explaining that Survey parties had fixed the main features in the 1970s but much of the remaining cartography was based on satellite imaging. He made a big show of the maps being "State Secrets" but to his credit he did allow us unrestricted access, which even the Americans had been denied. It would later prove fascinating to compare the real terrain, the maps and the satellite photos.

For the time being we had other preoccupations. According to our original timetable we would head south the following day. Unfortunately, said Huang, there would be a delay in Urumqi but we would make it up by flying to Charchan. The Chinese members would now number three and we might also have to take two radio operators. All expeditions had to take radios since the death of three climbers in the Tian Shan the week before. We hadn't brought the "micro radio" and Chinese radios were "very big requiring two operators to work them."

We left the final decision to the Chinese but the simple fact was that a radio would be useless. Regardless of our jokes at the press conference, once in the mountains we would be on our own and the chances of rescue minimal as our route would be too high and remote for helicopters and inaccessible for trucks. I was put in mind of Tilman's opinions on the subject;

> In my view every herring should hang by its own tail... anyone venturing into unfrequented and possibly dangerous waters does so with his eyes open, should be willing to depend on his own exertions, and should neither expect nor ask for help. The confidence that is placed, and successfully placed, in being rescued fosters carelessness or even foolishness, and condones ignorance.

The grinding reality of negotiations with the Chinese came as rather a shock to Tim and by way of light relief we spent the afternoon in the city centre. George was detailed to protect us.

Urumqi is an unlovely city, a sprawling dusty mess in the centre of an increasingly polluted plain. For several decades it has been at the centre of a virtually colonial expansion of Han Chinese immigration into Xinjiang. This has the twin objectives of exploiting the province's oil, gold and coal and diluting the native Moslem population. Originally, immigration was less than voluntary as Xinjiang was used as a penal colony, but in recent years the carrot has, at least partly, replaced the stick and George said he had volunteered to come to Urumqi after University. Like many he was now regretting it but permission to return east was harder to come by. In fact all the Chinese members of the expedition (excluding the camel drivers) would be Han immigrants, as was everyone we met at the Academy. Some had been trying to return east for thirty years.

The Han Chinese and the native Uighurs rarely mixed and generally the Uighurs were regarded by the Han as dangerous and unreliable drunkards. For their part the Uighurs together with the Kazakhs, Kirghiz and other minorities resented Chinese domination and occasionally showed it as we had seen in 1987. Violence was seldom far below the surface and this was one of the main reasons that the government was wary of allowing in foreigners. But the Uighur bazaars were the most interesting part of Urumqi and we dragged George into them promising he would be safe as long as he was with us. And he was, apart from one gesture from a passing Uighur casting aspersions on his virility.

"He is a loafer," explained George.

An evening chat with Huang suggested we would be stuck in Urumqi for several days. Our offers to help with preparations were politely declined and by the following morning my diary records that Tim had lost some of his urbanity and was "bordering on the irritable".

"I'm like the Foreign Legion – not good in barracks," was his comment as he paced his room – more caged bear than legionnaire. It wasn't the most interesting place to be becalmed but it was now unavoidable and I was surprised by his lack of stamina. I'm afraid I'd forgotten how unnerving the dead hand of Chinese bureaucracy could be on first encounter. Some sort of diversion was required and with a little prompting the Chinese eventually suggested we might like to visit Heaven Lake. We soon set out with George and Mr Zhou who was to become our regular driver.

Heaven Lake, nestling amongst the Bogda mountains about three hours' drive outside Urumqi, was a perfect antidote to the city itself. The mountains had been climbed by Shipton and Tilman in 1948 and more recently the lake had become something of a tourist attraction.

We drove out over the dusty plain, stopping for flat bread and kebabs in an Uighur café where Zhou knew the owner. Wherever we went in the next fortnight Zhou was sure to know the owner. Leaving the plain we climbed first through scrub, then green pastures and finally rocky outcrops before bursting upon Heaven Lake itself. In half an hour we had climbed through four climatic zones.

The lake was as beautiful as promised, surrounded by forests and snow-capped peaks with here and there an encampment of Kazakh yurts in a clearing. For verdant alpine beauty it surpassed anything we would encounter on the main expedition – but to my eyes there could also be a harder beauty in nature's wild and desolate places. We walked around the shoreline in the afternoon, passing a caravan of yurt-laden yaks waddling down to winter pastures, and retired to a dinky little chalet in the evening. Both sunset and sunrise were stunning displays and after a boat trip in the morning we were all sad to return to Urumqi – but looking forward to getting south.

The good news on our arrival was that the new route had been approved. The bad news was that our plane couldn't leave for another four days. I had quietly built extra days into our timing for delays such as this but I didn't appreciate Huang's exhausting them in one fell swoop. For his part Tim took the reverse stoically – well fairly stoically.

"I'm fucking appalled at the prospect of four more days in this hole. What it's like for the poor buggers who have to live here doesn't bear thinking about. I know you told me what it would be like but words cannot adequately convey the reality."

"Words cannot adequately convey..." became our second catch-phrase.

The following day preparations had progressed far enough for us to take stock of equipment. Tim and I had brought three geodesic tents and lightweight MSR stoves together with some dehydrated rations. The Chinese seemed impressed by the tents but obviously thought the stoves too flimsy. They said they would provide a fourth tent and another stove as the team had expanded. This stove turned out to be over a foot across, came with an even larger pressure cooker and fitted into a wooden packing case.

The contrast illustrated our different attitudes. Tim and I were still trying to keep weight down, partly, I must admit, because I hadn't fully revised the backpacking approach of 1987 to take advantage of the proposed baggage train. But we also hoped to retain a measure of freedom once in the mountains. The Chinese on the other hand completely ignored weight and planned to take everything but the kitchen sink.

However, it was clear that quite a few items remained to be collected. Huang's protestations that he had been preparing diligently for our arrival simply couldn't be true. When I taxed him on this he blamed the late arrival of both government approval and our payment for expenses – neither of which he had mentioned in his infrequent telexes. It was frankly a lousy start to the expedition and coloured everything which followed.

We next occupied ourselves with a day of cultural activities centred around a visit to the local museum. This was notable for a rogues' gallery illustrating the plundering of the Dunhuang Caves by, amongst others, Sir Aurel Stein. The display included the Chinese dust jacket of Peter Hopkirk's *Foreign Devils on the Silk Road*, the drawing showing shady silhouettes wearing Trilbies (obviously Europeans) and carrying spades. I didn't think it was a good moment to mention our part-funding by the British Academy Stein-Arnold Grant.

The climax to the day was a visit to the "Ali Baba Paradise" nightclub with a gaggle of Zhou's young female relations. These young ladies looked fourteen but were in fact in their twenties and a little light flirtation went on – strictly within the bounds of propriety, and in the interests of Sino-British friendship. The nightclub was a recent and unexpected innovation and like nightclubs everywhere, but possibly with more reason in Urumqi, it served as an escape from everyday life. We entered willingly into the spirit, Tim cutting a dash in the more decorous dances whilst I concentrated on the Uighur version of Rock 'n' Roll.

"William whirling dervish, indefatigable," notes Tim's diary.

Despite these diversions, time hung heavily. We were in Limbo. We filled the free hours with visits to the local market for steamed dumplings and demonstrations of tooth pulling, stopping off at the post office on the way. Tim seemed to have a compulsive need to keep in touch with his girlfriend (my own had long since despaired of regular contact) and when he described having repeated nightmares of bizarre animals I began to wonder if he was really suited to the expedition after all. But I needn't have worried – once out of barracks he would revert to his usual confident self.

On the day before our departure Huang announced that the plane had broken down and our journey south would be by truck after all. At least the radio operators weren't coming.

We gathered in the afternoon to load the trucks and were introduced to our third Chinese colleague, Wang Da Wei, a small, quiet but athletic physicist who would act as quartermaster. He would in fact prove remarkably efficient in the role but this was far from evident at our first meeting. After hours of confused inaction interspersed with intensive bouts of loading and unloading we were no further forward. I was for trying to organise the whole process but Tim rightly pointed out that such an approach would probably send me mad. We had to face it – for the time being we were in their hands.

The loading was completed early the next morning, our eventual departure in the Toyota Landcruiser being marked by a further surprise.

"Why don't you move into the spare seat, George?"

"Mr Wang will sit there."

"But Mr Wang is already in the back."

"This is another Mr Wang. We will pick him up shortly. We will have four Chinese members. Maybe this was not clear. Maybe my translation was bad. It is not my decision. I am only small potato."

"I am only small potato" was added to our list of catch phrases. By such trivial means did we keep sane. George invariably used it when he was instructed to translate something unpleasant.

The second Wang, Wang Hai, turned out to be an agreeable, rather hefty chap who was training to be a translator – but his main purpose on the expedition seemed to be as extra muscle. My first impression was of a westernised lounge lizard due largely to his affected sophistication. He was always keen to please the "honoured guests" but noticeably haughty with the surrounding populace, a common feature in China where everyone was friendly on a personal level but became a roaring tyrant given the slightest authority. As David Mathew had remarked,

"The principle is 'If you have a little power then wield it absolutely'."

There were now six of us in the Landcruiser, while Huang rode in the second vehicle, a Beijing jeep, with an Academy driver. Our route led due south (as indeed it would until we reached the Arka Tagh) first through an industrial wasteland then out over the southern plain beneath the snow-capped peak of Bogda Ola. Soon we passed a dormant forest of wind generators and, in the distance to the south, a camel train shimmering in the midday heat. The road was good, we were making fast progress and there was a festive air abroad with Zhou at its heart.

He was forty-nine, with a long, equine face and a voice to match. He had obviously driven westerners before, delighting in shouting,

"Let's go, Mr Joe," after every stop. He also had a way of circum-
venting official instructions "by accident". Huang obviously
regarded him as a disruptive influence but to us he was a welcome
blast of fresh air after the musty atmosphere of the Academy.

We stopped at Da Baiyanghe, a small roadside town, for lunch.
There was a tremendous kerfuffle to find a suitable place for the
"honoured guests" to eat in until eventually we found a tall arcade
surrounded by cafés and ate dumplings as the steam from cauldrons
of boiling mutton rose into the sunlit vault above. At the gate a
beggar chanted from the Koran, beating time with a staff hung in
chains.

Back on the road, the afternoon slipped away as we dozed
intermittently and woke to find desert alternating with dry
mountain gorge. Several times we were stopped at army check-
points.

"They are looking for social bandits," explained George. We
evidently didn't qualify.

As we approached Korla the desert fell back and high fields of
maize and sunflower enclosed the road. Here we stopped to buy
watermelons and sat in the shade of swaying poplars, spitting pips
into the gurgling irrigation channel. Korla was a smaller version of
Urumqi, mud huts rubbing shoulders with modern but already
dilapidated concrete factories. The guest house was in the latter
style and our stay was enlivened only by Zhou producing two
bottles of spirit at dinner. These had an astounding effect on
George, reducing him to a quivering wreck even before they were
opened.

"No, please, no," he wailed, shrinking from Zhou's outstretched
arm with every sign of abject terror.

He displayed the same pathological fear whenever spirits
appeared and not surprisingly came in for a fair amount of ribbing –
before finally being excused. I had read that some Chinese were
unable to digest alcohol and after hearing George's accounts of his
hangovers I had no doubt that he was one of them.

Korla marked the boundary of the area normally open to

foreigners, as we had found in 1987, and we were now to head across the Taklamakan desert into the "forbidden" area. Tim had dressed accordingly and drew admiring comments for his green bermuda shorts and hairy legs, neither a frequent sight in Xinjiang. As the jeep had fallen behind the previous day I suggested we should travel in convoy but this was rejected "because the vehicles have different speeds". It was anyway clear that Zhou was constitutionally incapable of holding back to travel with the jeep. On the few occasions we tried it some chance encounter would soon give him an excuse to forge ahead.

About two hours outside Korla we fell off the end of the tarmac road and started five days of intermittently choking, blinding and jolting progress south. At first the surrounding land was still cultivated and several times we passed soldiers "protecting" work parties in the fields. Then for a while we churned along beside the Tarim Darya, here little more than a muddy canal and shortly to disappear altogether in the shifting margins of Lop Nor. We disturbed a plover and later a buzzard from its banks.

Lunch was lamb and salt water tea at Tikanlik, a dusty halt where the lamb was hung in the centre of the room, for the convenience of customers and flies alike.

Gradually it became drier. Only a thin scrub remained, yet from time to time it was relieved by beautiful displays of purple and mauve flowers thickly packed on the radiating branches of tall trackside shrubs. I thought they were tamarisk but the colour seemed wrong. Botany was our weak suit.

Eventually the "tamarisk" and then the scrub disappeared completely. We stopped for a short break and climbing a nearby mound I looked out on the blasted desert that was the Taklamakan. It stretched unbroken in all directions, a flat sun-bleached expanse of sand, dotted here and there with formless mounds from which projected grey and lifeless twigs.

Somewhere beyond the eastern horizon were Lou Lan and Miran, long abandoned settlements excavated in the early years of the present century by our benefactor, Sir Aurel Stein. Here his investigations had unearthed a cornucopia of material pointing to strong Turkish, Tibetan and Chinese rivalry throughout the first millennium AD. His finds, like those at Dunhuang, had been carted off to the British Museum, the source of much later resentment by the Chinese.

Zhou's raucous "Let's go, Mr Joe," called me back and we pressed on. The track was still visible, its surface now churned into a fine deep powder which went through the cabin in billowing clouds. But the heat was stifling if we closed the windows and we saved this for the choking moment of passing oncoming trucks. As we wore steadily south these became less and less frequent. Zhou was in his element, keeping up a running commentary as he swerved from side to side, constantly searching for firm ground. George shouted that he was known as Zhou "Shifu", or Master Craftsman.

Hours went by and the desert surface changed again, rising on our right to form a sea of dunes, the track marking the eastern limit of their advance. Then, outlined dimly in the haze ahead, the Altyn Tagh mountains took form behind the approaching oasis of Charkhlik. A few minutes more and Zhou squealed to a halt in front of the municipal guest house.

This building's water supply and drains worked hardly at all and the lighting only intermittently but it did have a Great Wall Musical Pedestal Fan and Tim amused himself playing such Uighur favourites as "Greensleeves" and "Happy Birthday to You" whilst waiting for Huang and the jeep. They didn't arrive until late in the night, with the jeep chassis broken and radiator mounting severed.

In the meantime we had found the town's only bar and tried out our Turki. This caused quite a stir and the clientele crowded round to laugh at our hesitant efforts. We had some crib sheets provided by Tusun Yakup, our teacher in London, and were surprised to find that the locals could read them directly. Of course the Pinyin phonetic system which Tusun Yakup had used was the same which had been promoted by the Chinese in the sixties in order to destroy the use of Arabic script. However, for once the Uighurs had not been unfairly treated as the objective had also been to replace Chinese characters, Pinyin being seen as the key to faster learning and international advancement. Only recently had the policy been abandoned.

The morning discussion resulted unsurprisingly in our having to take a rest day whilst the jeep was repaired. Also a third vehicle was to be rented to spread the load. The jeep disappeared for welding and we had a look around Charkhlik (called Ruoqiang by the Chinese).

Once away from the handful of official buildings the tarmac soon ran out. We walked along a tree-lined avenue which had once formed the southern arm of the great Silk Road and plunged into a warren of baked mud houses and shaded courtyards heavy with fruit and flowers. Everywhere we went we were followed by the gurgle of irrigation ditches bringing the lifeblood of the oasis to the furthest corner. We passed a couple taking a grape-laden donkey cart to market, then suddenly two small children chasing hoops burst across our path. Had the daily life of the oasis changed since Hsuan Tsang had passed thirteen centuries before?

In the afternoon Tim and Huang went off to collect the jeep and the third vehicle. This turned out to be one of the most decrepit lorries I have ever seen.

"Huang says it's the best truck in the oasis but we'll be able to get an even better one in Charchan," reported Tim with barely concealed despair.

Our route the next morning led south-west along the Silk Road toward Charchan. We were travelling parallel to the Altyn Tagh but due to the distance and the virtually permanent sandstorm we glimpsed them only rarely. After a couple of hours we passed through Bash-shahri which, we were told, had once been the northern terminus of the route through the Altyn Tagh on to the Tibetan Plateau. For some reason all transport here was by ox cart rather than donkey. Then back into the desert. Where before there had been little traffic now there was none, yet a score of miles from the nearest settlement we came upon a lone lineman patiently sitting at the base of a telegraph pole waiting for a call. An hour later the truck stalled. We fixed the electrics and sent it on ahead but soon afterwards the jeep bogged down. By now the track had disappeared for long periods, and even where it was visible the powder surface was so deep that the desert on either side was rutted with attempts to find firmer ground. It was on one of these detours that the jeep had dug itself firmly into the ground.

We soon discovered that the jeep's four-wheel drive didn't work and probably hadn't worked since we had left Urumqi. Then we set to pushing and pulling and digging and swearing as both sun and temperature climbed. And all to no avail – after two hours the jeep was ten foot forward but even deeper into fine sand. The temperature had reached 101°F, we were beginning to resemble the desert around us and tempers were fraying. We weren't in any immediate danger – the Landcruiser was still working and we were on, or at least close to the main east-west route. Unfortunately the truck was somewhere ahead with most of our water and the route had no traffic. We had already tried towing the jeep with the Landcruiser without success but now we ganged up on Zhou, who so far had claimed the Landcruiser's winch wasn't suitable for the job in hand, and made him uncover it.

A more rusty, dirt-encrusted piece of metal it would be hard to imagine. It didn't give the impression of having been expertly serviced in anticipation of our arrival. In fact Zhou sheepishly admitted he hadn't opened the casing for the last four years. After a severe hammering and a liberal application of grease it was eventually coaxed into life but even then Zhou wouldn't use it as a winch. We simply pulled to better ground about fifty yards away and used the hawser as a long tow rope. With everyone pushing, and eventually falling flat, the trick worked and the jeep slowly juddered and slithered its way on to Terra Firma.

Another hour and another stop, this time for oil pump problems. I climbed a nearby dune and, laying down on the summit, came face to face with a rearing sand lizard. It looked as if it had lost its false teeth and intended to gum me to death. Luckily I had the advantage of size, as it was only six inches long. It scuttled away, perfectly camouflaged on the speckled sand. Meanwhile Tim had spotted a hoopo, (*Upupa epops*), a large bird with barred markings we were to see relatively frequently in the coming weeks.

The oil pump fixed, we pressed on as the desert became ever more featureless and barren. Then in the middle of nowhere we came upon a two-room mud hut which served as a café. We stopped for a lunch of noodles served on the *kang*, or raised platform, which here was surrounded by hanging carpets. The owner, a slim woman in her thirties was truly beautiful with a strong nose and cheekbones, silver-circled red stones in her ears and a lithe, graceful bearing. It was a haven of welcome surrounded by the desert and disturbed only by Huang and Zhou arguing outside about whether we should have stopped or pressed on.

In the afternoon we kept moving, but slowly. Added to the drifting the track was now washed out. The summer meltwater from the Altyn Tagh had carved great ravines across the route or in places simply swept the surface, washing away all traces of track. When water comes to an arid landscape such as this in a single yearly rush, the results are devastating. Zhou said that the road had been better three years before but floods and sandstorms had returned it to the desert. Here and there broken embankments and displaced culverts testified to unending and so far unavailing efforts to halt nature's advance.

Then as evening approached we were suddenly amongst lush green fields and poplars once more. We had finally arrived in the ancient oasis of Charchan.

Marco Polo had described the region in 1272:

> I will tell you of the next province of Turkestan, lying east-north-east, which is called Charchan. It used to be a splendid and fruitful country but it has been much devastated by the Tartars. The inhabitants worship Mahomet. There are villages and towns in plenty, and the chief city of the kingdom is Charchan. There are rivers producing jasper and chalcedony, which are exported for sale in Cathay and bring in a good profit: for they are plentiful and of

good quality.

All this province is a tract of sand and so is the country from Khotan to Pem and from Pem to here. There are many springs of bad and bitter water, though in some places the water is good and sweet. When it happens that an army passes through the country, if it is a hostile one, the people take flight with their wives and children and their beasts two or three days' journey into the sandy wastes where they know that there is water and they can live with their beasts. And I assure you that no one can tell which way they have gone, because the wind covers their tracks with sand, so that there is nothing to show where they have been but the country looks as if it had never been traversed by man or beast.

Unfortunately the passage of hostile armies has continued unabated to the present century, periodic insurrections against rule from Beijing and Urumqi alternating with the internecine feuds of local warlords. The history of the southern oases reads as a catalogue of murder, rapine, betrayal, execution and wholesale conversion to and from Islam. Only five months before our arrival the Chinese army was reported to have killed twenty-two Moslems in a pitched battle south of Kashgar and rumours of other revolts abounded. For the present the central Government retained complete control but it was, I suspect, eyeing developments over the former Soviet border with some trepidation. It is perhaps no surprise that one of the leaders of the Tien an Men demonstrations was a Xinjiang Uighur, Wuer Kaixi. He it was who humiliated the Prime Minister in a televised discussion prior to the massacre. He has since emigrated.

Our first duty on arrival was to meet the "Director of the Diplomatic Department of Qiemo County Government", Miss Wang, a plump Han exile done up to the nines in our honour. Her duties can't have been too onerous as the oasis remained one of the most isolated in the world, one moreover specifically prohibited to foreigners. Only a handful had penetrated thus far in recent years, two of whom, Nick Danziger and John Pilkington, had tricked their way illegally into the closed area. John had been somewhere hereabouts when I had been at the Gas Nor three years before.

After a shower in a nearby bath house, a meal and a good night's sleep we were ready to face negotiations. We soon realised that no one had any idea whether the camels were waiting as planned at Bash Malghun, the starting point of the expedition proper, and it was impossible to find out as the village had no telephone. We had to get out there as soon as possible but this was easier said than done. Miss Wang was being obstructive, the jeep had again disappeared for repair and the truck had started back for Charkhlik. The ensuing negotiations followed the familiar protracted Academy pattern and eventually resulted in Miss Wang deciding to accompany us to Bash Malghun in a new truck the following morning.

As we hoped to buy fodder at Bash Malghun, the only items to be purchased in Charchan were fresh vegetables and boots. The oasis was overflowing with fruit and vegetables of every kind, evidence of the desert's transformation by the waters of the now sluggish Charchan Darya. Like all the southern oases, Charchan relies upon the summer meltwater from the mountains for its very existence. Unaffected by the Indian monsoon these ranges receive only a tenth as much rain and snow as the Himalaya and, although further north, have higher snowlines. This comparative aridity largely accounts for the paucity of both vegetation and settlement and hence the difficulty of travel. But the meltwater from the high glaciers provides a brief river spate which enables the inhabitants of the distant oases to irrigate their summer crops. It has been suggested that the glaciers have retreated and the meltwater reduced over the centuries thus contributing at least in part to the abandonment of settlements deeper in the desert.

The other essentials on our list were to pose a greater problem. Impressed by the high-quality down clothing the Chinese had provided I had omitted to notice that all except Huang had no boots. As we had specifically paid for these it was yet another source of tension. A feverish search ensued and the quality of the resulting finds should have made us turn back immediately – but it didn't.

A century earlier Dutreuil de Rhins and Littledale had already formed their caravans before reaching Charchan. Dutreuil de Rhins had sixty-one animals including thirty camels to carry a total weight of seven tons yet even this was modest compared with Littledale's campaign.

Putting his determination to travel with adequate supplies into practice he had already purchased over eleven tons of fodder and six months' provisions. These including a quantity of cream which had been churned into butter by Mrs Littledale in Khotan then salted and soldered into tins for the journey. However even Littledale wasn't above last minute purchases and he had some metal tent pegs made in Charchan. It was presumably the same blacksmith who cut his silver ingots into smaller pieces as he was "short of change". In order to carry this mountain of baggage Littledale had engaged a caravan of two hundred and fifty horses, mules and donkeys, some of which would return once over the Arka Tagh. In addition there was a flock of twenty-five sheep which would act as a walking larder.

Both Dutreuil de Rhins and Littledale had also engaged guides. Dutreuil de Rhins could find no one who knew the route but he took with him Parpi Bai or Parpai, a seasoned traveller who had already accompanied Carey, Bonvalot and an unnamed Russian and had a reputation for having a wife in every oasis. Travelling two years later, Littledale at first seemed to have the advantage as he was able to engage one of Dutreuil de Rhins' camel men, Abdurahman, who supposedly knew the route. However Abdurahman turned out to be totally useless and was soon sent back with a minor injury.

Our own preparations complete, we spent the rest of the afternoon in the bazaar, the bustling heart of the oasis which spilled out into the surrounding tree-shaded avenues and alleyways. Here cheap clothes and trinkets from Pakistan and China proper vied for space with spices, silks and saddlebags from the southern oases. Roughly built booths lined the streets behind the stalls, each with a jeweller, barber or feltbeater plying his trade surrounded by an inquisitive audience. At the edge of the market oxen, donkeys, mules, horses and a lone camel waited patiently beside mountains of firewood. Wood was still the main fuel, although the cutting down of trees was now recognised as the most immediate cause of the desert's advance.

The streets were full with a noisy throng, young men in cloth caps rubbing shoulders with turbaned elders in long flowing robes. Only a few of the older women wore veils and the female population was almost universally handsome, clear-faced, round eyed and brightly dressed as far down as the knees where thick sagging stockings were *de rigeur*.

"An untapped market for suspender belts," mused Tim absent-mindedly. The Uighurs' appearance was almost European and, as if in testament to the ancient blood ties, we sometimes came across both men and women who could have passed unnoticed in any English county town.

Passing a tea house we stopped to try the local meat-filled pastries. The oven was a large clay urn heated over a wood fire, the owner leaning into its mouth and slapping our pastries against the inside wall. A few minutes later they were hooked out perfectly cooked and delicious. While waiting we had collected an inquisitive crowd which now drifted away in search of more exciting spectacle. Our novelty value at present was about five minutes.

Next the distinctive smells of roasting cumin laid an inviting trail to smoking kebab stalls where shafts of sunlight cut through the charcoal haze to pick out a corner of pink petticoat or flashing knife. At one stall I submitted to a laughing interrogation in Turki and Mandarin.

"Which country do you come from?"

"What is your name?"

"Arc you married?"

"Are you circumcised?" – this last in sign language, the stall holder finally realising that my vocabulary had neglected the subject.

The next morning we were up at six and off in the dark as the voice of the muezzin rang out over the oasis, calling the faithful to prayer. For two hours we retraced our route and then struck south towards the Altyn Tagh as Orion faded into the dawn. We entered the mountains along a wide dry valley which narrowed gradually to a twisting defile. When later it widened again Zhou leapt out with a whoop and stooping with both hands out before him ran across the river bed in hot but vain pursuit of a rabbit. Here we also saw a sand martin and some choughs. At the head of the valley we climbed a series of dusty hairpins and sat on the summit watching the jeep slowly follow behind us. The jeep was now unladen apart from Huang and the driver and was thus more of a liability than an asset. However, it seemed to be a matter of honour that it must reach Bash Malghun.

The Altyn Tagh were rounded and barren, with heavily incised ravines where the summer meltwater had cut into the hillside. We slid down the southern slopes to rejoin the Charchan Darya, here fast moving and deep at the bottom of a wide gorge. The river had cut successive deep channels, etching its ever-changing history in the soft gravel terraces of the valley floor. Whilst waiting for the others to catch up, Zhou lit a fire and we had a late lunch of hot bread. A weak sun glinted on the river tumbling grey-green over its stony bed. Beyond, the nine spurs of the Tokus Tagh plunged down to the far bank. When Huang arrived he pointed to our position on the map. I gently moved his finger eight miles to the west. This wasn't encouraging.

Our route led up the right bank of the river to the east. Soon we passed its confluence with the Ak Sou or White River where Dutreuil de Rhins had cut off to the south. The waters of the Ak Sou flowed out clearly into the muddy stream of the Charchan Darya. As the valley widened we left the river bank, climbed over a low spur and followed the southern base of the Altyn Tagh into a wide plain dotted with brackish bogs and grazing camels. Then turning away from the mountains we bumped across the plain and entered the last outpost of Bash Malghun.

We arrived in a cloud of dust to be greeted by a hoard of laughing, dancing children and an audience of no less inquisitive if more reserved adults. They were universally friendly throughout our stay and I was captivated. They reminded me strongly of the Tibetans I had met three years before, for they too had maintained an amazing vitality through adversity.

We were becalmed in Bash Malghun ostensibly whilst the camels were caught. In our first discussion shortly after arriving we were told they had already been collected but as we were late they had been released again. Since there was no radio or telephone link to the outside world they hadn't known what to do. Now they would take two days to prepare – two days which soon extended to four. The camels entered the growing list of subjects where we couldn't believe a word we were told. Once we were assured there were no camels in the village when we had just returned from counting forty in a walled enclosure. George tied himself in ever tighter knots trying to create sense out of sudden reversals such as this.

The grinding joylessness of negotiations was leavened only by the belief that we would soon be free of them and into the mountains – and by the idyllic tranquillity of our present surroundings. There was a timeless feel to life in the village and Tim came closest when he described it as Biblical. The low mud houses lined a single dusty street down the centre of which was channelled a narrow stream. There were few trees and the village was laid out naked on the plain, as if baring its soul to the vast heavens above. It had grown since Peter Fleming and Ella Maillart had arrived, exhausted, from the east in 1935. Then the village had had a handful of yurts, now it had several hundred inhabitants. In fact for a while I was doubtful if it was the same village, as the Chinese insisted on calling it Tura. Then the mayor explained that Bash Malghun had originally been the name of the village and Tura had been the surrounding area but when the scattered shepherds had been forcibly resettled together in 1962, the name had come with them. George, oblivious to his irony, said the present mayor had been "elected by the government". At over six foot tall he towered above his charges, his black beard lending a piratical air, although he appeared to rule by means of benign consensus.

The local economy revolved around camels and sheep. The sheep wool was hand spun and woven on a primitive narrow loom. A twenty-foot warp was first staked out on the ground and the weaving frame, supported on a tripod of rough sticks, was progressively moved along it, the weaver kneeling astride the finished cloth. We did see some coloured cloth but most was undyed apart from a simple brown/black geometrical pattern, each piece about eighteen inches wide.

For such a small village it was remarkably well appointed, with a lighting generator, a one-room general store, a cobbler and more than one house which doubled as a café open to all. Here we ate three good meals a day, devouring lamb in vast quantities and many guises – stewed lamb, lamb dumplings, lamb and noodles and a host of variations, each one more delicious than the last.

Each afternoon we roamed across the plain, its extent seemingly elastic as the surrounding mountains refused to come nearer. Bleached in the sunlight its gravel surface and sparse grazing nevertheless held sudden surprises – a wagtail, a lizard, a red dragonfly, then suddenly the Charchan Darya itself, wide and

Salt crystals

powerful, its course constantly shifting between crumbling banks. Away from the river shallow salt pans were criss-crossed by stick-like six inch crystals and dotted with clumps of sharp bladed yellow grass. For a while we were confused by the knots tied in the larger clumps until one of the villagers explained that they gave a purchase for tethering camels.

Close to the village a few small fields surrounded by raised banks provided grain and fodder. It was harvest time and in a scene which melted even our cynical hearts, singing families were cutting and stacking corn. The women glittered with gold piping in their dresses and jewels in their hair, even when working. Meanwhile the donkeys were staked out to manure the neighbouring plots. The fields were the toilet of the animals, the villagers and ourselves alike – and a more dramatic toilet it would be hard to imagine. Only the widespread hooves of the donkeys' defunct companions served as a reminder of the harsh realities of village life.

To the east the plain rose to a distant saddle, a route which would eventually lead to the Gas Nor, the scene of my 1987 debacle. The plain was in effect a continuation of Przhevalsky's Valley of the Winds. Over the centuries this had sometimes seemed to present an alternative east-west route to the Silk Road, but the altitude, lack of settlements, and difficulty of the terrain had prevented its being widely adopted.

To the south were the Musluk Tagh, our first obstacle, rising in ever higher ranges to a snow-capped horizon whilst to the north the Altyn Tagh, nearer and more dramatic, changed hourly as the sun moved across their heavily eroded grey flanks. They rose to a single snow peak opposite the village. One day we walked to the monu-mental ramped scree at the base. It was a world of giants, their fleeting shadows rippling over the mountainside, across the inclined tableland and down to the plain below. A low wind pulsed across the surface as though the plain itself were breathing.

Eventually our camel drivers appeared. These were Abdullah Kanje and Hassim Adje. Abdullah, the Caravan Bashi or head camel driver was dark haired and weather-beaten with a blue

domed hat. He also wore a superb pair of fur-lined suede boots at
this first meeting but although he took them on the expedition they
rarely surfaced and he made do with canvas plimsolls and puttees in
all but the coldest weather. He immediately put me in mind of
Sancho Panza. Hassim was short and squat but was fashioned from
iron. They were both in their forties although Hassim looked older.
It was later explained that they had only agreed to come because
they were poor, Hassim having only recently married. But first
impressions were good and we greeted each other in the traditional
manner, grasping the other's hands as though praying, intoning
"Salaam" and standing back whilst stroking our beards, or at least
the first vestiges of our beards.

Abdullah surprised us by revealing he had already taken a couple
of Americans, a father and son named Hilton or Hinton, to look for
the snow leopard in 1988. They had managed to cross the foremost
range, the Musluk Tagh, before being turned back by deep snow.

Now the whole party was collected we went through our route.
This would lead south over the Musluk Tagh to join the Ulugh Sou,
an affluent of the Charchan Darya, which we would follow to its
source. We then hoped to find a new pass to reach the headwaters of
the Kara Muran and finally climb the Kara Muran Davan onto the
Tibetan Plateau. The first half more or less followed Littledale's
route but we would have to play it by ear from then on.

Huang was worried about the reported lack of water on our
planned route through the Musluk Tagh and suggested we cut
through the mountains by following the gorge of the Charchan
Darya instead. We readily agreed but Abdullah was loth to try the
gorge and we had to drop the idea. We also reluctantly agreed to
drop the final foray on to the Tibetan Plateau due to the delay in
starting. The Kara Muran Davan would be our ultimate objective.

How much Huang was to blame for the pathetic advance plan-
ning we didn't know but the subsequent organisation was obviously
proving too much for him. Unfortunately he resisted our help in
overcoming problems whilst simultaneously denying there were
any – the wish becoming confused with the reality. Truth is a

variable commodity in China at the best of times and in Huang's hands it was proving almost infinitely flexible. But such is the Chinese obsession with "face" that any criticism was bound to make matters worse and we were left to enter into the charade and massage his bruised confidence at every reverse. I was torn between regret for having suggested him as Joint Leader and conviction that it had been the crucial factor in retaining his interest and thus in our obtaining permission where others had failed. We would just have to live with the consequences.

At least Tim and I were still on good terms, an important consideration after my 1987 journey. He had been rather downhearted after Zhou had disappeared with our last letters home, but had otherwise regained his confidence and was as desperate as I was to get into the mountains.

That night the mayor invited us to a *tamasha* or party. This started unpromisingly late when we filed into a dingy room in the mayor's quarters and sat on benches behind empty tables. Then flat bread appeared, then beer, then mounds of roast lamb and we set to with a vengeance. Finally despite protests by the Chinese, bottles of Arak, the local firewater, were produced and the speeches began. First we were welcomed and toasted by the mayor then Huang did likewise and not to be outdone I made my first and only speech of thanks in Turki.

"Sanga man kandak rahmat eytixhi bilmayman. San manga bak qungkur tasir kaldurdung. Man sini manggu untup kalmayman."

Tusun Yakup's instruction had proved its worth.

The toasting continued, first the mayor and "toastmaster" encouraging the guests to down their glasses in turn, followed by a return engagement when Tim and I went through the Uighur ranks. Miss Wang, who had briefly replaced Huang in our demonology, was attending as an "honorary man" and couldn't escape this process, receiving a particularly large tot. She downed it, turned green and retired, to be next seen the following morning, slumped in a truck bound for Charchan. We were doubtless ungallant but I plead mitigating circumstances. Her one raison d'être appeared to be to delay our departure as long as possible and her considerable bureaucratic skills had been wholly devoted to this end. Things looked up after she left.

A final surprise awaited as Uighur music blared from a tape recorder and the toastmaster invited Tim to dance. I was just thanking my lucky stars for a close escape when the Mayor presented his compliments and whisked me on to the floor. The traditional circling dance, hands held high, was followed by a waltz and the evening wore on in increasingly tipsy confusion. Da Wei had already sloped off, George was excused spirits and Huang entered half heartedly into the proceedings but it was Wang Hai who now came into his own, looking happy for the first time since leaving Urumqi.

"I like drinking," he beamed.

The rest of the evening is rather hazy but I have vague memories of Tim toasting the Stornoway Gazette. His diary omits this but inexplicably accuses me of "dancing excessively". It was, of course, mere politeness on my part. We spent the next day recovering and preparing the loads. Compared with Littledale and de Rhins we were being positively frugal with only a ton and a quarter of fodder and three quarters of a ton of provisions and equipment including three freshly slaughtered sheep. Even so the weight had grown since our original estimates and, allowing for the human supercargo, our nineteen camels would be carrying about 300lbs (135kg) each at the start, well over the supposed maximum of 220lbs (100kg).

We also assembled and tested the stoves. Our MSRs seemed weak and the Chinese model was proving troublesome but Huang unveiled a secret weapon in case of emergency – an industrial blowtorch which roared like an inferno. It wasn't our idea of lightweight camping gear – but it was going anyway.

Then as night approached, a herd of bellowing camels were led into the village. They were great shaggy beasts, all but two frail make-weights looking heavy, strong and ponderous. Each fixed us with an imperious gaze as it passed. Their spindly legs, the rear knock-kneed, led down to feet the size of dinner plates, each divided into two pads. The front feet were largest, supposedly the sign of good breeding. These were Bactrians, two humped camels, the humps coming in all shapes and sizes from erect and full to flacid and lopsided. At Abdullah's urging I thrust my hand into the neck of one camel. It sank into a soft deep pile, perfect insulation for the journey ahead.

Now Abdullah and Hassim set to fixing the saddles. One by one the camels were couched. Most had noseplugs driven through the side of the nose, just below the nostril and with a tug at the halter attached to this and a harsh "Chuga, Chuga, Ch, Ch, Ch" from Hassim the complaining camel first knelt on its front legs, its hocks rising bizzarly in the air. Then its rear feet crept forward until it could sit, and finally the front legs did the same until the animal was horizontal. Now viewed from the rear the beast's hard skull and small ears had a strangely Neanderthal appearance. Next the saddle was formed of two flat straw-filled sacks, one either side of the camel. A wooden staff was placed along each sack running fore and aft and fixed tight into the body with ropes at front and rear and between the humps around the camel's girth. These saddles would remain in place until late in the expedition, even when the loads were removed. With saddles fixed the camels were bedded down outside our window to gurgle and belch their way through the night.

'The wind-footed steed is broken down in his speed, whilst the camel-driver jogs on with his beast to the end of his journey.'
(Quotation from Sa'di in 1258)

CHAPTER 5

Stampede

Off at last only eight days late. After the false dawns of the last ten years, riding a camel south out of Bash Malghun was in many ways the most satisfying moment of the whole expedition.

The morning had opened with what can only be described as a Festival of Loading. We still had no idea how to go about this, although it would come in time, but today there was no problem – the whole village turned out to help. Infants only two years old were delegated to hold the halters whilst greybeards too old to load gave the benefit of their conflicting advice. For the next two hours the courtyard in front of our quarters was transformed into a ferment of dust, bellowing camels and straining villagers as one by one the beasts were couched and the baggage tied on. Then felt mats were laid over the top of the baggage to form a platform on the riding camels. Abdullah and Hassim had red flowered quilts in lieu of felts and in this they had the best of the bargain. When all was packed Hassim completed the final touch, tying a fifteen pound bell round the last camel's neck. The bell had a camel-bone clapper, no doubt "pour encourager les autres".

We took a late breakfast and the whole caravan trailed out to the edge of the village to pose for photographs. I had a vision of a neat rank of camels in line abreast with the expedition members in the foreground, but I was to be disappointed. The camels weren't so co-operative and of course the whole village wanted to get into the act, pushing and laughing as we tried vainly to organise proceedings.

Finally, everyone had had their fill of photographs and the camels were couched. Under the amused gaze of the assembled village we straddled our beasts for the first time and tried to look suitably relaxed as they struggled to their feet and, at a sharp whistle from Hassim, set off across the gravel plain to the south-west.

We travelled in two strings, Abdullah leading Huang, Da Wei and George whilst Hassim led myself, Tim and Wang Hai. The baggage camels brought up the rear. For the first time since we had reached Bash Malghun the weather had closed down and we started in a thick mist, hardly able to see from one string to the other. By now I almost expected some last minute personnel changes and I wasn't surprised to find that Abdullah's dog, a burnt sienna mongrel called Seyn, had joined the expedition. I wondered how she would fare in the high mountains but for now she was happy as a sandboy, or possibly sandgirl, racing ahead and scouting the route. Below us the ships of the desert rose and fell with each step as hanging on grimly fore and aft we tried vainly to ride the swell. Through the swirling mist the doleful toll of the camel bell warned of dangers to come. I half expected the Eddystone Lighthouse to rear up on the port bow.

It was even more disconcerting when, half an hour after starting, the bell fell silent. The last camel had come free from its halter and stood silently while we pulled ahead. Unconcerned, Hassim dismounted and walked back to collect it, tying on again for the first in many scores of recaptures.

The mist lifted slightly as we reached the banks of the Charchan Darya. In the course of the expedition we would cross and recross this same river many times, but here, midway between its source in the Arka Tagh and its destiny in the sands of the Taklamakan, it was at its fullest. Luckily the summer spate was receding and the river had split into several channels which could be taken in turn. One by one the camels slipped down the shallow bank and into the water, heading slightly upstream to combat the rapid current. To my right Tim fought desperately for handholds on the mound of baggage gyrating wildly below him. I had little doubt that I presented a similarly ridiculous sight. Slowly the water rose to the camels' bellies, yet they held their feet and we pulled across, clouding the downstream water as we passed.

The land on the far bank was a complete change. Although it looked the same flat plain from a distance the ground was covered by a low moss which was completely waterlogged. The surface swayed at each step and the camels became skittish, hating the lack of secure footing. This continued for the best part of an hour before we reached the southern edge of the plain and turned right skirting the foot of the Musluk Tagh. When later the mountains turned north we continued straight on and plodded slowly up an arid sand saddle. Looking back our tracks showed as a dusty white line stretching to the plain before disappearing in the mist beyond. Our umbilical cord was finally severed.

After breasting the saddle we started across a short enclosed plain. I had been following our progress on the satellite photos and shouted to Tim that we should soon turn south. It was lucky that Abdullah knew this part of the route for it would be another day before we made the turn. I had completely misjudged our move-ment over the photo. I felt a complete fool but much of map-reading depends on familiarity and I salved my wounded pride with the knowledge that I was familiar with neither camel riding nor navigating by satellite photo. What in Britain we had assumed were narrow valleys were in fact wide valleys and what we had read as wide valleys were veritable plains. We knew the factual scale of the photos, but translating that onto the ground would take time to learn.

At first even distinguishing mountains from valleys was difficult but this became much easier when I made a chance discovery – I held the photo upside down with south to the top. As the photos were taken in natural sunlight the light side of the mountains was therefore to the south, now upwards and the shaded side to the north now downwards. The human eye, certainly my human eye, appears to be accustomed to light coming from above, i.e. the sky, and by revolving the photo in this way I found the mountains and valleys sprang into three dimensions. Gradually our skill improved and we came to identify major features and judge progress with a fair degree of reliability. Trying to keep them in focus whilst lurching ten feet above the ground was another matter.

Hassim looked back and, seeing my contortions, showed a gap-toothed grin. Then as we loped across the plain he launched into a high-pitched song, half wail, half lament, although for all I knew it was a joyous celebration of freedom.

We descended from the plain through a steep defile, so narrow that our baggage banged against the sides. On the steepest sections Hassim blocked the route with the lead camel, moving forward one camel length at a time until each succeeding camel had glissaded down. At the bottom we came out into a wider scrub-filled valley and camped on a terrace overlooking the confluence of two small rivers. Our initiation had taken five hours and we had covered about twelve miles. Below us the main river broke through the mountains to the north to join the Charchan Darya. The smaller river, which Abdullah called the Kirruk Ungur, was the valley we would follow the next day.

We pulled into camp in single file and couched the camels. Abdullah and Hassim showed how to loosen the ropes and let the loads fall – a matter of only a few minutes. Assuming we would want to stack the baggage I grabbed a hundredweight sack of fodder and humped it to the centre of the terrace. Hassim split his sides laughing as I fell to my knees totally exhausted and fighting for breath. The effect of the altitude, here only 10,530 ft (3,210 m), was astounding.

Ten minutes later when I had recovered Hassim explained by sign language that my laudable efforts had been totally wasted. All loads except those needed for the night's camp were left where they fell. The next morning the camels were led into camp in the same order into the same positions and the loads were ready to hand for tying on. I didn't make the same mistake twice.

Without a word spoken Tim and I busied ourselves with the tents whilst the Chinese went down to the river and started cooking. After hobbling the lead camel and freeing them to graze upstream, Hassim and Abdullah sat munching bread and watching the camp take shape around them, their work done for the day. Thus was set a precedent which was followed with little variation until we returned to Bash Malghun.

Tim and I shared a tent, Huang and Da Wei a second and George and Wang Hai the third, leaving Abdullah and Hassim with the Chinese tent. There was no escaping the second-class nature of this item. A blue ridge design, it looked suitable for a light summer weekend in the south of England and took ages to erect. The zip was constantly breaking and the pegs bent double at the slightest caress. But what it lacked in strength it gained in size and probably because of this Abdullah and Hassim professed themselves perfectly pleased. Our own small yellow and green Quasars performed admirably and with the felt mats and sleeping bags in place were a perfect home from home.

Seeing Huang labouring to scratch out a cooking pit, Tim unpacked a folding shovel, an item of which I had been blissfully unaware.

"I knew you wouldn't approve, so I didn't tell you," was Tim's full explanation. Being of equable temperament I didn't complain and the shovel proved invaluable in digging pits for cooking and rubbish, and just occasionally for erecting tents. But I wondered what other surprises were hidden away. Were we, like Peter Fleming, carrying a wind-up gramophone and a stock of records?

After erecting the tents Tim and I went for separate walks. This wasn't due to any falling out but seemed to come quite naturally as a sort of implicit statement of independence. I was rather pleased with the fruits of my walk, a brown speckly phallic growth found pushing through the nearby sand, but it was eclipsed by Tim's discovery. Returning to camp he dumped a dead snipe in front of the tent with the triumphant air of a gundog retrieving a grouse. He was cock-a-hoop at the find, or at least as cock-a-hoop as Tim ever allowed himself to become and we speculated that it might be a new species, soon to be named Snipus Martinimus. Later research suggested a Pintail Snipe (*Gallinago stenura*) on its autumn migration from Siberia to India but it was at least the first sighting in the region. We had already seen an eagle, a hawk and a dipper earlier in the day and were to be pleasantly surprised throughout the expedition by the amount of birdlife which survived here, the snipe being a notable exception. Of course it was the season of the autumn migration and many of the birds we would see in the coming weeks would be in passage rather than resident.

Huang hallooed to announce food was ready. This sticky mess of boiled rice, carrots and lamb was a great success. We threw the bones to Seyn but she kept her distance, especially, I noticed, from Abdullah. We had round flat bread and brick tea with the lamb. The bread had been baked in Bash Malghun and we had a sackful. We were still finishing it weeks later but it was by then a trifle hard. The tea was full of stalks but convenient, a few slivers being shaved into the kettle at every meal.

Camp 1 was an undistinguished camp, the sky was overcast, the mountains around were dusty and the valley was a mess of scrubby terraces, but to me it was close to paradise. It meant we had started and for better or worse were cast on our own resources. Tim and I had our aches and pains but we seemed to have survived the first day's riding with no permanent injury and, tired out, soon fell asleep.

We were awoken by Abdullah noisily brewing tea. Slowly the camp came to life, Tim leading our own turgid resurrection. It was cold outside and the tent throbbed to our attempts to don warm clothing before emerging. Half an hour later as the sun rose above the surrounding peaks we were forced to shed the hard-won insulation layer by layer. Breakfast was the night's congealed left-overs followed by a second pot of tea. We set about lowering the tents, whilst George and Da Wei cleaned the pots. After a while Abdullah and Hassim started off to collect the camels and in the fullness of time these were brought into camp and couched in the same positions as the night before.

Even with the loads beside the camels loading was a heavy job which fell largely on Abdullah and Hassim. Wang Hai helped Hassim and I spelled him from time to time when my conscience pricked. The loading was easiest with two men, one holding the bags in place beside the saddle whilst the other tied the ropes in a simple but critical sequence, first under the belly and between the humps, then fore and aft around the saddle poles.

We were ready to leave four hours after rising, a period invariable throughout the expedition – our attempts to speed up the process by organising simultaneous cooking, tent demounting and camel collecting being met with studied incomprehension. Abdullah made it quite clear that these activities were ordained to be carried out one after the other and a herd of stampeding yak wouldn't induce him to believe otherwise. He explained that a camel could, in any case, only travel for a limited period each day and it might as well be in the afternoon after an unhurried start. This seemed an unanswerable argument and we soon fell in with the local usage, insisting only that we complete a full day's march once loaded.

Huang fell off his camel as it rose from its haunches (always the most dangerous moment), putting a great strain on our good manners as the whole party fought to stifle its laughter. I was pleased to see we had left the camp more or less as we had found it. We had agreed with Huang that refuse would be burnt and buried and toilet areas would be sited downstream. It seemed to work and we avoided both litter and diarrhoea until we were back in civilisation.

Our route led up the Kirruk Ungur to the west. The summer meltwater had cut a deep ravine in the flat floor of the main valley and as we followed the remaining stream our view of the surrounding mountains was obscured for hours at a time by the shoulders of this lower incised valley. Twice I was sure I heard the call of a sand grouse in the earth banks above us but I could see nothing except a few holes. It didn't seem outside the bounds of possibility as Ella Maillart had found a sand grouse nest further east – and made an omelette.

"The most delicious dish of the whole journey, a landmark in the history of the expedition." Peter Fleming had gushed.

Unfortunately, Tim had not heard a thing and his opinion of my ornithological descriptions was so low by now that the sand grouse was consigned to the "possible" list.

We had been going for about two hours and were crossing the stream for the umpteenth time when one of the baggage camels held back, pulled its noseplug halfway out and bellowed the rest to a halt. Hassim walked back to fix it, giving a double click through his teeth which invariably meant, "Come here while I do something unpleasant to you."

The process seemed painful for the camel and dangerous for Hassim. To start he took a precautionary turn of rope around its muzzle but as soon as he tried to move the peg the camel gave a high pitched wail and swivelled a gangrenous set of teeth towards his outstretched hand. It took half a dozen attempts before the deed was done and we could set off again.

Every day on the march was punctuated by regular stops such as this to tighten saddles, tie halters, fix noseplugs or simply repack recalcitrant baggage. Tim had a theory that the Chinese nylon ropes we were using slipped more than the softer homespun ropes to which Abdullah and Hassim were accustomed. These were still used for tying on the saddles and one or two other jobs and they did seem to give less trouble. But in any case halters were never tied too tightly between one animal and another as it was preferable for the animals to come loose rather than pull out nose plugs. As in other aspects of camel management, the halters appeared to be of psychological rather than practical use.

Gradually the river inched round to the south and the incised valley took on a greater importance, its sides becoming deeper and more rugged. So far we had been following Littledale's route and now we were joined by that of Dutreuil de Rhins. Ahead, a watery sun glinted in the stream as we climbed. Together with a gentle breeze it made the afternoon pleasantly warm. But both sun and breeze were deceptive. Already, after only two days my face and lips were burnt and swollen, and the backs of my hands were cracking open. Too late I started to cover up.

We camped as the sun dipped below the western horizon. By now the valley had become a gorge and our camp was pitched on a flat terrace about thirty feet above the river. Here everything about us was encrusted with salt, from the surface of the terrace itself to the river banks below which were hardened into a succession of flat stalagmites. Salt flavoured our food and tainted our water and was probably the reason that my rucksack buckles had started to jam closed. The buckles weren't the only casualties. As we wrestled with them on the terrace above, flares and explosions suggested that all wasn't well in the galley below. Having successfully disciplined the buckles, we sauntered down to watch the Chinese stove in its death throes. Two nights of coaxing by George and Da Wei had failed to find its soft spot and it had never lasted more than two minutes at a stretch. It was duly consigned to the rubbish pile or, more precisely, it was carefully re-packed in its wooden box and carted along until we could convince Huang to leave it in a depot nearly a week later. It was obviously still regarded as a considerable asset.

Now the much maligned (by us) blowtorch came into its own and was to do sterling service for the rest of the expedition. The system was, of course, the same as a petrol stove, only the shape being different, but the critical factor was obviously its simplicity of operation, as both the Chinese stove and our own MSRs pretended to a higher level of sophistication and delivered a higher level of uselessness.

Later that night I climbed the slopes above camp to watch the moon rise over our own lunar landscape. It was moments such as this that I enjoyed most of all but as the silence of the stars drew me on, the belch and clatter of camp life held me with an earthly tether.

The next morning Huang was immobilised by a headache. It was possibly a sign of Acute Mountain Sickness but he revived after a couple of paracetamol and we started in the early afternoon, only slightly delayed. We stopped to fill our large water bags at the river as we were approaching the waterless part of the range. Whilst they filled easily if held in the current they were surprisingly unwieldy once full and flopped around like gigantic sausages attempting an escape.

The gorge first increased in height then widened out as we climbed and, as predicted, the river eventually disappeared into the sand. The whole landscape was much more arid than I had expected and the scale much larger. We were obviously on a well used route by local standards and passed several dry stone cairns in good repair. We also noticed a metal tripod topping one of the flanking mountains. George's claim that it was a survey point seemed a trifle credulous to our sceptical minds. The tower was well over twenty feet high and we secretly suspected it was a military communications relay. We were to see another couple over the next few days and then they disappeared.

Twice the bell camel sat down on the job until pulled upright and the third time he lay down on his side. Hassim beat him savagely around the muzzle until he rose, by which time he was bleeding copiously from the nostrils. I remembered Wilfred Thesiger writing in *Arabian Sands*;

> I have never seen a Bedu strike or ill-treat a camel. Often I have watched my companions fondling and kissing them whilst they murmured endearments.

The Uighur way with camels was different and relied more on fear than love. Yet from time to time some sign of concern and rugged mutual respect would surface. For our part I'm afraid we held our counsel, treating the camels as well as could be managed but not trying to overturn the whole basis of the Uighurs' control. In time I became quite attached to my own camel, a feminine beast with soft golden hair and long eyelashes I named Dawn. Only later did I find he was a castrated male.

As we climbed out of the gorge our view opened to reveal distant snow-capped peaks on all sides. For hours at a time they hardly moved as we rode silently over grand terraces along a shallow valley, here several miles wide.

Towards evening we parted company with Littledale and Dutreuil de Rhins whose routes struck off to the left up a broad valley leading to the Zarchou Davan or Gold Washers' Pass. It took several hours to cross the end of this majestic valley and as sunlight gave way to snow the valley floor was painted in wash after wash of subtly changing hue. It was an altogether more savage prospect than the picturesque beauty of Heaven Lake, but one which I found wonderful in its desolation. These immense solitudes thrilled by their uncompromising austerity.

We pressed on to the south where, Abdullah said, there was a second pass unknown to the earlier travellers. But soon after passing the junction he stopped to make camp in the centre of the valley floor – just as the wind began to rise. It was about as exposed a position as you could hope to find and I couldn't see the sense of it. I wasn't alone and after a strained discussion we went on for another hour towards the flanking mountains where we camped under the lee of a steep spur. We never did find out why Abdullah and Hassim preferred to camp on exposed sites. Water didn't appear to be a factor, as tonight there was none and on other occasions rivers meandered from valley side to valley side. Maybe to the Uighurs the mountains represented danger from wild animals. Even Bash Malghun, I recalled, had been placed almost dead centre in the Valley of the Winds.

It was already dusk by the time we had pitched our tents so we made do with tea and a cold meal.

"We have big treat tonight," said George proudly brandishing a large pack of tinned anchovies. Surrounded by a salt-encrusted landscape at a dry camp it was just what we needed.

The camp was not only dry but also largely devoid of grazing, so the camels were fed grain for the first time. Once the loads were untied the camels were shooed off into the valley whilst two canvas sheets were layed out and covered with a half bag of grain each. At this the camels came thundering back to cluster round the sheets, the strongest to the fore. The whole process was extremely messy as they trampled grain, earth and each other underfoot. Fights broke out and the weaker brethren eventually had to be fed separately. To make matters worse after the first night it was difficult to keep them from the sheets as the grain was poured but as before Abdullah and

Hassim regarded the system as immutable and carried on regardless.

I spent the rest of the evening wrestling with my camera which had now succumbed to the all pervasive cocktail of salt, sand and dust and was refusing to wind on. Eventually it seemed cured at the cost of a wasted film but the same problem was to recur throughout the expedition just at those moments when I was about to take an award-winning shot.

I had a disturbed night, waking repeatedly to the fine breathless crackles which certainly were "audible without a stethoscope". Thoughts of mortality were seldom far away in the grandeur of our increasing isolation and now supplied with a focus they came to the fore. I had had too long to dwell on the rate of attrition amongst earlier travellers to the area and to research the facts on Pulmonary and Cerebral Oedema, each complications of Acute Mountain Sickness. Virtually the whole expedition would take place in the altitude band where most oedemas had been reported and whilst the risks were normally slight, I was less sanguine than my doctor about my periodic wheezing. This had been put down to a miscellaneous allergy but if so I must have been carrying the mysterious irritant with me because the wheezing had continued all the way across China, a fact I had taken care to hide from the Chinese and, as far as possible, from Tim. It seemed an undesirable state in which to start such an enterprise. Maybe my fears were the product of the anchovies swimming in my brain, but they were real enough and it took a conscious effort to overcome them. Luckily the compensating urge to complete unfinished business was too strong to resist.

Meanwhile Tim too was keeping his own counsel and only later confessed to having had serious bouts of breathlessness, nausea and anxiety. He too overcame them.

The temperature dipped below zero for the first time overnight and ice formed in the cups outside the tent door but by the time we started at noon the sun was blazing and the temperature had shot up. It was Wang Hai's turn to part company with his camel at the start, the cause of rather more laughter than concern. Hearing this,

Wang Hai seemed more worried about the damage to his pride than his behind. Our route lay southward along the wide dry valley towards a snow-capped peak which looked increasingly daunting as we approached. It was easy to see why Dutreuil de Rhins and Littledale had felt it best to strike off east a day earlier.

Seyn meanwhile had started a hare and we watched the two sunlit puffs of dust as she pursued it over the still-shaded valley sides. The hare always won, in this case building up an unassailable lead and disappearing over the crest of a spur, pausing only to thumb its nose at the flagging dog below.

After an hour we struck off first east up a cul-de-sac then south again up its flanking hills. Another first was marked when we had to dismount and climb on foot up to a low saddle. From now on the spells of walking and scrambling increased sporadically until they replaced riding altogether. The climb wasn't particularly steep but it was long and dusty and hot and both men and camels took it very slowly. At the top we paused for Huang to take the first of many "Victory" photographs and surveyed the land ahead. Directly in front the high snow-capped peak rose on the far side of a wide dry valley. This was the same valley we had left earlier and we had simply cut the corner as it turned eastwards in front of the peak.

The saddle proved just as tiring to descend as it had been to climb, the sun beating back from rocks bordering the faintest trace of a track. At the base we remounted and sauntered east up the main valley under the lee of the snowy peak. Now the sun's rays were tempered by a light breeze and life seemed very pleasant. Tim and I amused ourselves by taking Lawrencian photographs of each other as we lounged more or less confidently recumbent on our swaying mounts.

Although dry the valley was far from lifeless. Spiders scuttled and lizards swirled and a brilliant orange butterfly raced past in a hurry. And high above the valley's ramparts an eagle wheeled in the blue depths of the sky. Finally, as we approached the skyline two small troops of kyang (*Equus hemionus kiang*) or wild ass broke for the cover of the flanking mountains, chased a mile behind by Seyn in hot pursuit.

The watershed when it came at 14,270 ft (4,350 m) was hardly noticeable. We were still flanked by high mountains and it was only the gradual rising of a distant panorama which told us we had reached the summit. This was the Wolf Pass. We now looked down a continuation of the same valley towards a distant plain bounded on the far side by an unbroken range of snow-capped peaks. I took several bearings to the highest points, which were almost due south, in the hope that I might later identify them but as we descended they were soon obscured by the mountains on our right. Huang was intrigued by my Silva compass and borrowed it for a while. At the time I assumed it was to compare it with his own but it soon became clear that he didn't have one. In fact George was the only Chinese who did carry a compass. I was about to ask if he had been specially chosen for this pivotal role when I remembered that the last telex had asked us to bring "two have many function compass". I decided I had better keep quiet.

Gradually the mountains on our left receded and we found ourselves marching down a massive inclined ramp towards the plain below. Pace by pace the reflection of the sun from the ground intensified until eventually we were loping across a whitened salt pan.

"Monotonous," grumbled Tim.

"Travel in Asia is not a dance upon the dropping petals of the rose," I responded, quoting Hedin.

"Hmph." He gave me a withering look, his opinion of both Hedin and myself only too evident.

Later the camels became restless as we followed the shore of a shallow lake. Hassim grimaced to show it was salt water, his gap tooth giving him a roguish air. Several times the lead camel made towards the lake and was hauled back by Abdullah. The water certainly wasn't a matter of life or death – but our mounts' keen sense of smell coupled with the dry fodder of the night before made the lake irresistibly seductive. A little further on we passed a freshwater spring gurgling from the base of the mountains on our right. Hassim dismounted and put his lips to the spout to test it, then gestured that there was better water ahead. He remounted and we pressed on round the next headland. But it was more than our beasts could bear. Just round the headland the last five camels of Abdullah's string suddenly broke free and, bucking wildly to dislodge their loads, started galloping back to the spring. The result was pandemonium as the rest tried to follow, rearing, bellowing and strewing baggage over the plain in a scene reminiscent of a wild west rodeo. Abdullah and Hassim started to run after the escapees whilst the rest of us dismounted and struggled to control the remainder.

When calm was restored we began to walk back to the spring and Tim held one of the less determined escapees. But once caught it regained its determination and back legs flailing, convinced him to let go again. We regained the spring only to find that three of the camels had kept on towards Bash Malghun with Abdullah in pursuit – so we decided to camp, retrieve the fallen baggage and await their return.

After pitching the tents, Tim and I climbed the low col behind camp and sat enthralled as the setting sun daubed splotches of apricot and purple across the darkening plain.

"Magnificent," admitted Tim, "Maybe travel in Asia is a dance upon whatever it was after all."

Abdullah arrived after dinner leading three very chastened camels.

The next morning, Sunday, Tim roused me with his version of "The Morning Service" not I think from any great Christian zeal but rather from homesickness. Unfortunately he couldn't quite capture the correct flavour of unctuous cant to make it thoroughly convincing.

Our first discovery on emerging from the tent was to find that the three camels had disappeared again during the night and Abdullah was out tracking them. Their flight was no doubt aided by the time-honoured method of restraint which again owed more to psychology than common sense. When necessary each camel had been tethered to a small rock or other handy package which until now seemed to have convinced them that they couldn't move. However, they had now realised that they could carry the burden along with them and several camels were presently wandering the camp each proudly dangling its rock like a treasured jewel. I politely suggested that in future we should use a more substantial weight.

Whilst waiting for the (hopefully) recaptured camels we basked in the late morning sun and discussed the route ahead. This now led south-east to the valley of the Ulugh Sou and meant crossing the desert plain we had first sighted from the Wolf Pass. All went amicably enough until Huang announced that he and Abdullah wanted to divert eastwards to rest the camels where there was good grazing. This after starting a week late and completing a mere four days travel! Following the disingenuous shambles of the last fortnight, it was the last straw and I exploded.

He should exchange his hat with Abdullah if the camel men were going to dictate terms, I declared. They had no interest in risking themselves or their animals to reach the Arka Tagh but I expected Huang to show a bit more determination. Conserving our strength was fine but we had to balance it against the rapidly approaching onset of winter and further delay would only increase the risk of being caught by the weather. Had he no grasp of timing? Or did he, perhaps, imagine we would turn back short of our goal? If so he was sadly mistaken and the sooner he realised it and pressed on south the better. Announcing the discussion was at an end I stomped off quivering with residual anger into the desert.

My outburst was hardly likely to nurture Sino-British friendship but it did have the merit of a certain cathartic honesty. And it had touched on the crucial problem – Leadership. Many times I found myself hankering after the near absolute powers of a Littledale or Hedin but it was impossible. Even the official 'Joint Leadership' of Huang and myself was a simplification of the position on the ground for in reality we had a three-way Chinese-British-Uighur split of power. Unfortunately our attempts at co-operation which worked so well on a day-to-day level, broke down as soon as we started discussing progress and routes. My decreasing and already low confidence in Huang's organisational abilities and his increasing resentment at what he saw as my overbearing attitude were not to make for a placid passage.

Meanwhile Tim had been left with Huang – "feeling rather like a lemon," he said later. Eventually he went for a walk of his own around the next headland, where I met him later stalking geese beside a salt lake. We had also seen a flight of ducks and a hoopo earlier whilst performing our ablutions. We walked back to camp together, arriving at the same time as Abdullah and the camels.

It was mid-afternoon by the time we had made ready. We started by climbing over the nib of the mountains behind camp and crossing the dry bed of the Toghru Sou river. This was done very gingerly with Abdullah dismounting and showing every sign that he expected quicksand. He seemed to regard the whole area including the salt flats as very unreliable country. I was sure some of these 'dangerous' sections were pure theatre but in the absence of knowing which were theatre and which were real I followed his line religiously.

The crossing successfully achieved we set off across the desert. I was relieved to find Abdullah was heading south-east as we had originally agreed.

We aimed for a range of low hills shimmering in a dusty haze on the far edge of the desert, a tantalising vision which was to stay at a seemingly constant distance for much of the day. We were over 14,000 ft (4,300 m) high and noon was long gone, but the temperature kept on rising, soon reaching 80°F (26.5°C) as we moved out onto the exposed plain. The sun beat back from the hard gravel surface, burning and cracking any exposed flesh. My head throbbed dully in time with the mournful toll of the camel bell and I took out my glacier glasses. They made the desert bearable but once on it would be impossible to remove them until dusk. Hour after hour we crawled over the perfectly flat surface, the two strings always the same distance apart, tied by an invisible thread.

From time to time the gravel faded into hard sand but there was no other relief, not a plant grew, not an animal moved, except Seyn who came in close to trot in the shadow of the camels. Over to our right whirlwinds swept down from the jagged snow-capped peaks we had seen the day before. Then marching across the desert, they flung themselves on the pink hills ahead and vanished.

After four hours we threaded between crescent dunes and crossed the barest trickle of water sliding over the plain. This had been our original goal for the first day but Abdullah and Huang in the first string had passed on and could be seen in the distance, still holding to the south-east. Huang had resolved to recoup the face lost that morning and exhausting the camels was one way of proving his point. The fool had decided to cover the two desert stages in one day.

We pressed on. As the day cooled and the still heavily-laden camels flagged, we dismounted, our shadows surging and lengthening before us as we walked from the setting sun.

We had remounted and were climbing the lower slopes of the dusty hills by the time we came up with Huang and Abdullah. Huang offered a contradictory selection of excuses for passing the stream but we both knew it wasn't meant to be taken seriously. However, now was not the time for recriminations – night was falling and we needed to find a campsite, preferably with water.

Abdullah seemed to know the country and, promising water ahead, he led off diagonally up the slope towards a shallow saddle on the skyline. The route became steadily rougher and as the darkness thickened about us the camels stumbled and reared, dislodging stones which clattered into the void below. Finally they baulked at one particularly acute corner and we dismounted again, leading them by the light of our head torches onto the saddle above. Then with Abdullah still swearing there was water a little further on we descended the eastern slopes, our eerie caravan clanking slowly downward, lights and shadows flashing far into the night. Caught in the beam of the torch, the camels' footprints appeared raised above the surrounding sand, the beasts depositing

Kebab stall in Urumqi

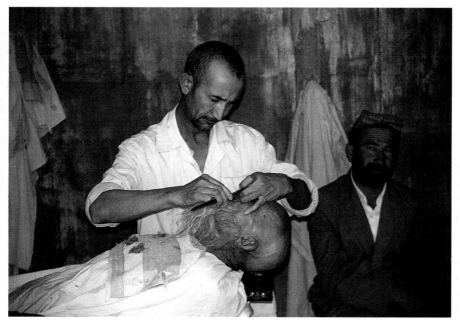

A nose amputation in Charchan

In Charchan

George

Arrival in Bash Malghun

At Bash Malghun, Altyn Tagh in distance

Narrow loom weaving, Bash Malghun

Abdullah

Nose Plug

Loading

Our first crossing of the Charchan Darya

Hassim leading between Camps 3 and 4

Camp 6

At Camp 6. Our first distant sighting of Ulugh Mustagh

Tim after an argument with his camel

Glacier Camp

Seyn

Blizzard at the lake

Number 3 resurrected

Exhausted

The lake. Camels on the spur and Seyn a dot on the ice

Tim with Ulugh Mustagh in the distance

Surveyors' Camp

Abdullah and Hassim at Surveyors' Camp

In the gorge of the Charchan Darya

Skull on the Musluk Pass

The Musluk Pass

Looking down the gorge of the Charchan Darya

a small mound from hollow legs with every step. I remembered the TV interview in Hong Kong – how prescient Tim had been. We only needed to fix our head torches on the camels and the nightmare would be complete.

Eventually we rounded a small headland and Abdullah called a halt. It was nearly midnight and we had travelled 20 miles, the last five in darkness. Our camp was the site of the promised water but there was none to be found. We erected the tents with difficulty in a foul temper and ate a disgusting offering of dry powdered meat before falling exhausted into a bottomless sleep.

Snipus martinimus

CHAPTER 6

Ulugh Mustagh

We rose to find we had camped in the dry bed of the Ulugh Sou. Maybe Abdullah had been here in a different season. We had a reconciliation with Huang over breakfast, pledged undying friendship between our Two Great Peoples and set off south-east across the river bed.

The valley was about four miles wide at this point, the surrounding arid hills containing a flat floor marked by the imprint of a hundred shifting channels. No doubt two months before, these would have been a formidable obstacle but now in mid-September they were dry. The banks were pockmarked by the holes of small rodents which scattered as we approached.

Shortly after starting we saw our first antelope but the chances of getting close seemed remote. Our only hope was to come upon a strain which was both deaf to the tolling of the camel bell and blind to Seyn's holy terror of a dustcloud which was even now racing across the plain. Of course she had no chance of catching them but the chase was the thing and when she eventually tired she rejoined the caravan, strutting jauntily and bragging, "Don't worry, I've seen them off".

Turning south up the valley we came first upon tiny rivulets of ice, then at last upon a shallow channel of water which paradoxically gained in volume as we moved upstream.

Soon we found ourselves moving through the centre of a colony of marmots, (*Marmota bobak*, or possibly *Marmota himalayana*) fat dog-sized rodents, all reviewing the march past with a critical eye. Seyn was continually frustrated in her attempts to catch them as they left it until the last minute before diving into their sets. She ran from mound to mound as they popped up and down like a fairground game.

We called a halt after a short stage just as half a dozen wild yak, (*Bos mutus mutus*) filed away over the western skyline. Camp Six was in the centre of the valley, below a shallow terrace beside the main river channel. The camels were loosed to saunter off in search of grazing. It looked poor stuff – isolated tufts of orange grass dotted across a plain of gravel.

We had now rejoined the routes of Dutreuil de Rhins and Littledale. Having crossed the Zarchou Davan they had followed the valley of the Ulugh Sou from the three river confluence where it joined the Toghru Sou and Musluk Sou to form the Charchan Darya. Littledale had had a lucky escape whilst fording the river near the junction.

> While I was on horseback in mid-stream helping a man who was trying to save one of our animals which was being carried down the stream, a piece of ice struck my pony behind and we were carried down 50 yards before I could get clear; the animal, fortunately for me, kept his legs, for the water was bitterly cold.

Littledale had pressed on southward but Dutreuil de Rhins had left Grenard somewhere near our present position whilst he ransacked the south-western mountains for a passable route. He had returned to find one of his men, Musa, ill with "an inflammation of the chest" and when the Frenchmen headed south again, Musa was allowed his discharge and sent back to Charchan.

We relaxed for the rest of the afternoon and tried our Turki vocabulary on Hassim. Suddenly Tim ran for the binoculars.

"Isn't that a wolf?" I looked at the grey-ochre shape skulking along below a terrace about six hundred yards away.

"No it's Seyn."

"Oh – I'd forgotten about Seyn." We relaxed again.

"But Seyn's over there with the camels."

Sure enough Seyn was over to the left about the same distance away, and we could now see that the wolf was twice her size and lighter, grizzled brown with a grey stripe across the shoulders. It was stalking the camels, travelling, tail low, along the base of the terrace and rising now and then to peer over the edge. Suddenly it caught our wind or Seyn's, froze for a moment then turned and loped off unhurriedly to the north. Tim was ecstatic in a Tim sort of way – and I was fairly pleased by the sighting myself.

Littledale had come across wolves but on the other side of the Arka Tagh. Even then he had only seen their effects. One night his sheep had been allowed to stray from camp and the following day the whole flock were found in a shallow valley with their throats bitten out but no meat taken. The caravan man who found them cut out the kidneys for Mrs Littledale but the rest was left behind.

Later Wang Hai said he had seen a full pack of wolves in the distance to the north. We didn't imagine they would do us any direct harm but we did make sure that our mutton was well protected overnight. In many ways we were better provided for than our predecessors but unlike them we didn't carry a rifle and wouldn't be able to shoot game in an emergency. Unless of course Tim had packed one with the folding spade.

The camels did in fact become restless during the night and Tim went out to investigate, finding nothing unusual. Even so we were careful to cover the food from now on.

We agreed to a rest day at Camp Six and the following morning Tim and I set out for a hike along the valley. We soon spied five antelope in the distance although as they were hornless we thought for a while they were kyang. We stalked them for half and hour and got to within about 400 yards before they spooked. Luckily for them we were only armed with cameras. However, lacking a really long lens and a fortnight's wait in a hide our wildlife photography was universally poor. At least that's my excuse.

Determined to get closer to the subject, I turned my attention instead to a colony of marmots. There was no chance of taking them by surprise as they had been watching our antics from the sidelines, so I just glued the viewfinder to my eye and walked straight towards them. They sat imperturbably on their mounds, front feet raised and noses pointing disdainfully in the air until I was about fifteen yards away when they dived into their holes. You could almost hear the klaxon sounding – "Dive, Dive, Dive". But my subtle ruse had worked and the resulting photograph was one of the few where the subjects were actually recognisable.

In the afternoon we lounged around camp, fixing equipment and reading, accompanied by Da Wei playing selections from the Sound of Music on his harmonica. Da Wei himself had continued quiet and competent although the initial impression of athleticism had been marred by his shuffling flat-footed gait and unrepentant chain-smoking. There had been no formal announcement but he seemed to be regarded as the Chinese second-in-command, or even the power behind the throne. This wasn't impossible as China still operated a dual technical/political leadership at all levels. One night I even dreamt of a leather-jacketed Da Wei drawing a revolver when we refused to take the approved route.

Da Wei didn't play often and George was our main music maker if his repetitive wailing of Auld Lang Syne could be called such. Sadly, my own wide repertoire of whistling was now silenced by swollen and cracked lips. I could tell that Tim in particular was saddened by the loss.

There had been a few wisps of snow earlier but now it was warm and sunny. I sat in the door of the tent catching up on my diary.

"Doesn't talk too much, is generally easy going and knowledge-able, just enough faults to be bearable," is the relieved entry on Tim. Outside he and Seyn dozed in each others arms watched by an inquisitive wagtail. The mountains to the west stood back from the river and we were enclosed by a circle of rounded slopes, each covered in rivulets of cascading snow. Beyond them jagged snow-plastered peaks peered through a rolling mist. A flight of geese went over in formation, the sun catching their wings as they dipped. Above, white-edged clouds ploughed across the blue depths, casting running shadows on the land. A bee buzzed past the tent heading downstream – it was altogether too relaxing and I dozed off.

A cool breeze blew up as the shadows lengthened and we all slowly came to life. All except Wang Hai, who had disappeared for a solitary walk. By now we had revised our earlier superficial impression and he seemed much less confident – although still with pretensions to sophistication.

"I find eating with the hands uncivilised," he had confided. This was unfortunate as we would spend much of the expedition gnawing large hunks of lamb, our beards and clothes eventually becoming congealed with a thick mixture of mutton fat and dust. George said Wang Hai was henpecked at home but he obviously missed his wife and young daughter and wasn't used to being away for so long. I thought it unlikely that he was a willing volunteer. His heart wasn't really in the enterprise but he tried his best and, removed from the necessity to protect the honoured guests from the locals was always very good natured. We managed halting conversations about his family and our life in Europe but his English was not as good as George's, "I think you are right," being his invariable response to our questions. On the other hand his lack of confidence forced me to try my Mandarin whereas George's competence made me lazy.

It was surprising how well we all managed to understand each other. Abdullah spoke some Mandarin and Huang managed some Turki – although not as much as he imagined, Abdullah and Hassim often standing bemused as he regaled them with hearty back-slapping banter. He also spoke a little English to supplement George and Wang Hai. And of course there was my basic Mandarin and our stock phrases of Turki. The rest was sign language. We did sometimes have misunderstandings but I suspect most of these were on purpose.

Wang Hai turned up as I was cooking dinner. This concoction of kebabs, cumin and rice was my contribution to the general wellbeing and seemed a success although I was crestfallen when Da Wei started to cook an extra dish of hot peppers.

The MSR stoves were proving fairly useless at this altitude, 14,270 ft (4350 m), taking nearly an hour to boil a kettle of water. We tried all three together which gave a marginal improvement but by then they were using as much petrol as the blowtorch. This was a frightening amount and our rapidly diminishing fuel stocks were already giving cause for concern.

Taking a few early morning photographs the next day I looked up the valley and was electrified by the sight before me. There was Ulugh Mustagh, The Great Ice Mountain, a pure white pyramid shining in the morning sun, with a second peak like a shadow beside it. Even at a distance of 40 miles the peak looked majestic and daunting. It was just where I had looked for it the day before but it had been obscured by cloud. As I watched the cloud closed in once more. In the darkest days of the eighties I had promised myself I would be satisfied with this single sight of the range – but of course once achieved it only whetted my appetite for more.

We started up the bed of the Ulugh Sou more or less in the centre, crossing and recrossing the river. We now appeared to have passed the limit of Abdullah's knowledge although it was always difficult to get a clear idea of his travels. He had stopped somewhere to the north when guiding the Hiltons or Hintons two years before. Huang had also been close on the 1984 expedition. This had used jeeps and, as the Musluk Tagh were impassable, they had taken a long sweep across the Achik Kol Plain to the river confluence. But when attempting our present valley they had been forced back by floods.

Soon after starting we disturbed four Orongo antelope, (*Pantholops hodgsoni*) each with magnificent horns, long, very slightly curved and twisted like a barley sugar. They bounded off towards the mountains.

An hour later we halted and Abdullah started to leave a depot of fodder and provisions. As we were still supposed to be returning by a different route this caused us some consternation. I could smell another acrimonious row brewing but to my surprise it wasn't between Huang and myself. A few sentences into the translation George took off on his own and for the next 20 minutes he and Huang stood nose to nose shouting at the top of their voices, spittle flying, whilst the rest of us sat waiting for the storm to subside. Wang Hai and Da Wei scuffed their boots in the dirt in an embarrassed sort of way whilst Abdullah and Hassim effected total disinterest. Tim and I were very interested but taken aback by the turn of events.

I assumed George was complaining that Huang was devious and Huang was telling him to shut up and obey orders, but truth to tell I couldn't follow the drift and Wang Hai's explanations were purposefully vague. All attempts to bring peace were rebuffed and it was simply a matter of waiting until they ran out of steam. Then a sullen silence reigned for another five minutes and we broached the matter of the route. At first Huang tried to use Wang Hai as translator but this soon proved unworkable and he had to revert to George.

"Mr Huang says other route will be longer," reported George, "Abdullah does not think of future like Mr Huang and uses too much fodder. Maybe Mr Huang was wrong about our last talk. He thinks we should leave some things here and come back this way. I only repeat what he says. I am only small potato."

It was Huang's turn to be surprised when we agreed. We weren't pleased at the further slicing off of our objectives, but Tim and I had come to much the same conclusion. We had decided we must concentrate on our major objectives: crossing first the new pass beside the icefield and then the Kara Muran Davan. We left four sacks of grain and some petrol at the depot, well covered, and continued up the valley.

From a distance in the watery sunlight the valley sides appeared faun and the river bed grey, but the colours were made up of a Pointillist canvas of yellow grass, green pebbles and pink earth. It was far from dull close up. There was also a wealth of wildlife on the valley sides, particularly Orongo antelope and black herds of wild yak which made off as soon as we came within a mile. Then a thirty strong troop of kyang appeared on the spur above us and watched our ponderous progress before sweeping over the skyline in a swirl of dust. They were lithe, slim beasts and it was easy to confuse them with antelope from a distance. Given the poor grazing they must have had a massive range to survive. In fact the number of animals in such desolate country was amazing. The ground was literally covered in tracks, some of which, I suspected, were months old. Once the surface crust was broken, the effect of wind and sand seemed minimal. Certainly our own tracks could be seen clearly three weeks after they were made.

We climbed the valley sides when the terraces became too steep and then slipped down again to follow the valley floor. Several times an hour we had to climb or descend terraces anywhere from six to sixty feet high. Descending was worst, the main danger coming just after the first camel had led off. We always came to the edge at an angle and instead of following the lead camel's line the others were apt to turn sideways and stampede down the slope in line abreast, rather like the Indians in a western, but with less heed of what lay at the bottom. By now we took such events in our stride. On the flat we had abandoned hand holds and often found ourselves dozing on the march, swaying in time to the gentle swell of our camels' gait. The grind and squeak of their teeth, the soft patter of their pads and the creak of chaffing ropes had become part of our lives. And unconsciously we had become accustomed to our own mounts, the ride of the others seeming strange by comparison. But they all travelled at an almost invariable speed of two and a half miles per hour. This increased marginally as the loads decreased and we were averaging a respectable fifteen miles a day compared with the six to seven miles of Littledale's admittedly more cumbersome caravan. However the altitude and lack of grazing were already taking their toll. The camels' humps were growing smaller and thinner each day and their dung came in small hard balls instead of the fibrous green piles we had seen at Bash Malghun. We had also come to recognise the different temperaments of the camels. One or two were belligerent, others timid, but in the main they were co-operative enough. Even so it was well to avoid the rear legs of all our beasts. They could deliver a vicious and unexpected punch if anyone strayed into the danger zone. The lesser danger at the front end was to be covered in camel spit and regurgitated grass. Tim looked rather like a field of stubble after one such incident. The camels rarely fought but when they did each would attempt to bite the humps of the other, usually the front hump. Abdullah and Hassim treated them warily at all times but insisted on having the last word if any camel disobeyed. Apart from tugging on the noseplug and beating with the halter the final sanction was a large rock thrown at the neck from point blank range. Small wonder if the camels took their revenge when it offered.

Late in the afternoon the valley detoured to the west around a rocky promontory. Possibly due to the deviation Littledale had struck off up a wide valley to the west, no doubt imagining it was the easier route. In the end it had cost him dearly in both time and animals as he threshed around in the surrounding ranges before finally finding a route south. Dutreuil de Rhins had also attempted a westerly route, with similar results. We had yet to see if we would fare any better on the new route.

We followed the main valley as it resumed its southerly course and soon after came across the remains of an old camp where we halted for the night. It was a surveyors' camp from the nineteen sixties or seventies and all that was left were a few bamboo poles and some broken pottery. Presumably it had been used as base from which to cover the surrounding area. So far the maps had been thoroughly reliable on those features, unlike the river course which could be considered fixed, but from now on they were to prove less so.

George refused to explain the cause of his argument with Huang, saying only that he didn't like "working with stupid people". Under the circumstances I didn't think he meant Tim and myself. His willingness to argue with his leader was unusual in itself in the strict Confucian hierarchy of Chinese society, and I hoped it wouldn't catch up with him on our return. George said it didn't matter, he worked in a different department from Huang and would speak his mind. Considering he was constantly in the awkward position of having to translate unwelcome news he was bearing up remarkably well. He was looking rather less clean cut by now, his hair striking an attitude of continual surprise, possibly at the appearance of a few straggling escapees on his lip and chin. We were still trying to understand each other's sense of humour – with a notable lack of success. George always laughed in the wrong places. Maybe we did too. Despite this he stayed chirpy and was eager to learn about our lives. But he was definitely the baby of the party – the others called him "Che, Che" – and sometimes betrayed a touching naivety about the outside world. His main sources of information to date being old television series and the Voice of America radio, he was rather shocked by our mixed reviews of life in the west. Yet it couldn't be denied that we lived lives of relative freedom and comfort compared with George's spartan and regulated existence. He told us of his life in the Academy, his room mate, his family in the east and his hopes for the future. These now revolved around returning east and if possible travelling abroad to complete a higher degree but both were unlikely to be permitted. We talked about the events in Beijing and George said all his friends had been interested but of course they were "non-political" – a wise choice at the time. I didn't press him further. It was an ironic barrier to friendship with those we liked most that we were loth to draw them into dangerously incriminating discussions.

Sheets of ice floated down the river as we started out the next morning. Then as they cleared, Ulugh Mustagh and its surrounding icefields came out of the cloud and hung at the end of the valley for the rest of the day. The icefields and buttressing mountains were extensive although their boundaries were masked by the shoulders of the nearer slopes.

We headed steadily southwards, then followed the valley round to the west, the snout of the closest glacier slowly rising above the valley side and then slinking back as we approached. Forward progress in relation to the surrounding mountains was virtually imperceptible. Upward progress was actually imperceptible. Only the passing stream of the Ulugh Sou showed we were gaining height. Swathed on my camel I worked it out. We were gaining about 600 ft a day, or 100 ft an hour on average, or 1 foot

8 inches a minute, or one inch every three seconds. Slowly but inexorably. Towards dusk we pulled into the mouth of a small tributary and camped under the northern lee of the mountain.

The temperature fell steeply as we pitched the tents. Combined with the increasing wind and altitude it was making life much more difficult. All tasks took longer, from the tying of knots to the digging of pits in the rock hard ground, and the gentle banter of camp life slowly declined. After dinner Huang and Abdullah came asking for headache pills. Huang had also broken his glasses and we fixed them with string and wire. He didn't have a spare pair.

Tim and I usually stayed awake for an hour or so after climbing into our sleeping bags. The reflection of our torches from the yellow tent and red bags gave a relaxing glow and we would write our diaries or fix equipment whilst finishing a mug of tea. We had both brought worthy tomes and read a fair amount, although Tim was finding it harder going with *Ulysses* than I was with Sartre's *Roads to Freedom* – and he was usually the first to suggest a game of cards. Apart from the single night on the Yorkshire Moors it was the first time we had shared a tent and it could have been disastrous – but it wasn't. We had different backgrounds and were interested in each other's stories and opinions – often coming to a similar outlook by different routes. We had both travelled largely alone in the past, Tim in Europe and Africa, myself in North and South America, but so far we were finding each other perfectly bearable despite the increasing demands on us during the day and the worsening dust and smell in the tent at night. I suppose it was because we were both such good-natured, easy-going and essentially friendly people. On the other hand we were both finding it hard going to withstand being part of the larger Sino-British expedition.

I was first awake the next morning, not a usual occurrence, and after making a brew and failing to rouse anyone else I clambered up the slope behind camp for a better view of Ulugh Mustagh. From here the twin pyramids looked ridiculously pure and symmetrical, their rocky summits giving way to steep snow slopes whose edges glowed in silhouette before the morning sun. The snow slipped easily down to the glaciers below, eventually running out onto the brown foothills across the valley. It was too cold to be still but I pottered around on the low headland above the camp, happy to be there and alone for a few moments, until inevitably the sounds of reviving life drew me down again.

As before our route followed the Ulugh Sou. It was smaller now but iced over and the camels recoiled from crossing. Slowly we coaxed them onto the surface but it was only a crust and gave way with a "Crumph", causing even more alarm as they subsided into the icy water below. Luckily it wasn't deep and we crossed without mishap, pushing our way on the far bank through a mound of dirty snow which had survived the summer melt. Now the valley widened and divided, the junction opening up a sweeping panorama of snow-capped mountains on all sides. The junction itself was dominated by an inclined red cliff which climbed diagonally from the valley floor to the northern skyline above us. The right-hand valley rose grey, arid and sandy to the west. On the far side of the distant saddle lay the routes of Littledale and Dutreuil de Rhins. But we had agreed to try the left-hand valley – as yet an unknown quantity. The stream of the Ulugh Sou led up this to the south, eventually disappearing behind the distant spurs.

We followed, calling to each other and pointing out possible routes west up the flanking mountain slopes. Sooner or later we would hit the glacier at the head of the valley and if we couldn't then continue south we would have to retrace our steps. These slopes would be our second alternative. They rose in layers, each range higher than the preceding until the whole massif culminated in an extensive snowfield or possibly icefield. Even starting would be difficult as the summer meltwater had cut into the base and the lowest hundred foot or so was a sheer wall.

As we rode south the two peaks of Ulugh Mustagh travelled with us, sliding along the eastern skyline. I took bearings when the two summits came into line. Two hours later the eastern slopes fell back and we found ourselves riding across the crumbling face of a massive, heavily-crevassed glacier. Further back the glacier split, one branch climbing east and the other south, the two frozen streams bracketing the north-west face of Ulugh Mustagh.

It took an hour to cross the glacier front. We kept on south along the main valley which now narrowed, the meltwater terraces becoming closer and deeper. Seyn tried to climb the flanking slopes but fell back defeated. The terraces rose higher above us melting into the valley sides as they also closed in. A cold blast came from ahead. Our way now seemed blocked by a high rocky barrier, yet there was a key. Urging our beasts forward we entered the stream itself and followed its icy thread between echoing walls into the hidden world beyond.

This new world was a world of ice. Emerging from the defile we were confronted by a shining white wall over a hundred feet high and stretching from valley side to valley side. Its face was deeply marked by crevasses and chasms, their depths lit by a dim blue-green light. Curtains of icy lace hung from the surface, reaching down over marbled pillars and massive slabs like tapestries in a frozen temple. At the base the Ulugh Sou slid silently from a tunnel of snow.

We set up camp about forty yards in front of the face. It didn't seem to be calving and we imagined we were relatively safe. It was only when we were juggling with the tent poles that I looked up and saw the glacier really did have a face – a central prow with the face of a solemn elder crevassed into its surface. He would watch us sagely during our stay, steaming in silhouette as we rose every morning.

It was still only late afternoon and after a hurried discussion we convinced a reluctant Huang that we should reconnoitre our intended route. The three of us with Abdullah, set out on foot.

We headed along the right-hand edge of the glacier as we looked at it. It was, I suppose, strictly the left bank as the glacier

flowed down the valley. First we had to climb up the slope above
camp. Then we worked our way along the mountainside parallel
to the glacier. The ice cliff which formed the glacier front continued along the edge and formed a cleft where the mountain
dipped below the glacier. This cleft was more or less V-shaped
with the left hand of the V the near vertical ice face and the right
hand the marginally less precipitous mountainside along which
we were clambering. The mountain itself was heavily metamor-
phosed and made up of millions of flat schistose sheets from the
smallest leaf to large jutting boulders set at crazy angles. In
places whole rivers of razor sharp vertical blades flowed down
from the slopes above whilst nearby it was possible to pick individual pages from tomes of flaky white Muscovite. We each took
our own line and I gradually pulled up the mountainside away
from the glacier face. At the top of the sheer edge a pure white
blanket rolled back to the horizon but as the surface was convex,
it was impossible to see further than the first few hundred yards.
Our progress was slow and tiring but the route had promise. We
started due south and slowly curved round to the south-west as
the glacier edge followed the mountain flank. Combined with the
repeated rocky spurs and shallow ravines of the mountainside
this conspired to prevent any long-distance views. The others had
stayed down in the cleft as I had worked up the slope to the
right, and when we reached a shallow col overlooking the glacier
face, I sat and waited for them to climb up.

Ahead was a grand amphitheatre formed by the semicircular
dip between two mountain spurs and the edge wall of the glacier.
A small pool of limpid green water trapped against the glacier
face formed the stage and the backdrop was the face itself, hung
with frail ice stalagtites. Above, the evening sun outlined the
brilliant white of the glacier surface against a blue-black sky of
snow-laden storm clouds.

Soon Abdullah and Tim appeared and we crouched watching
ripples spread out from the glacier face as the icicles melted. It
was a while until Huang arrived puffing at the col, but when he

did the effect was startling. He lay on his back and waggled his
legs in the air shouting "Victory, Victory", at the top of his
voice. The victory was apparently not his having reached the col,
but the fact that the route ahead was passable. Unfortunately
this was far from evident as the next spur was much higher, and
presumably followed by others higher still. But Huang wasn't to
be subdued.

Abdullah was less sanguine about the prospects and set off for
the next spur. The rest of us weren't feeling active anough to
follow and we lounged on the scree as he slipped down to the
pool and pulled slowly up the opposite slope. The round trip to
the horizon took over an hour by which time the sun had disappeared and the temperature was plummetting. Abdullah's report didn't sound encouraging but the only words I could understand were "big water". We hurried down to camp for George's
translation.

We couldn't have been too pessimistic because we had a snowball fight on the way. One of my bullseyes filled Tim's pockets
and he suggested I was lacking the gravity of a Joint Leader. It
was true, with the experience of the last few weeks behind me
and the challenge of the pass imminent I was enjoying life more
and worrying less. I still found the constant haggling over routes
wearing but as the going became more difficult I looked forward
to each day with increasing enthusiasm.

We discussed the "big water" over a lamb curry, one of Da
Wei's more delicious offerings which served to put us in an even
better frame of mind. This was just as well, because Abdullah's
news wasn't good. As far as we could tell from his confusing
descriptions, the route ahead was blocked by a lake. He was
convinced the pass was impossible but we couldn't leave it at
that. We decided that five of us (the same four as today, plus
George) would take unladen camels up the route the following
day. Wang Hai, Da Wei and Hassim would stay behind with the
rest of the camels and the baggage. Resolving to get an early start
we turned in for the night.

Sand lizard

CHAPTER 7

The Unknown Lake

The following morning we rose sluggishly and breakfasted on brick tea and the remains of the lamb as the first glancing stabs of sunlight showered down from the glacier face.

Presently, the small snowball which was Seyn detached itself from the larger snowball of her favourite camel and in parting they licked noses. Considering the foulness of camels' breath, I was amazed she survived. Maybe true love conquered all. Unhappily for Seyn this romantic state of affairs didn't extend to the rest of the camels, who regarded the dog with a baleful eye and delivered a hefty kick if she came in range. Often enough she spent the day limping along beside us, bloody but unbowed after a moment's lapse of attention.

Given our ignorance of the route ahead, Tim suggested that we take down and pack one of the Glacier Camp tents. Huang agreed but made it painfully obvious that ours was the chosen tent. When for good measure we threw in a stove, some food and a First-Aid kit he clearly thought we had overstepped the bounds of good taste and were being unduly alarmist. Our preparations evidently caused him an unbearable loss of face by implying that something might go wrong.

"Huang says there is no need to take these things. There will be no problems," reported George in his most non-committal voice. I settled for an air of restrained sanctimony whilst Tim bustled around muttering imprecations under his breath.

It soon became clear that he was engaged in a hunt for a further critical item of equipment and after a fevered ten minutes the quarry was finally unearthed. This turned out to be Tim's pride and joy, an old sheepskin trapper's hat with large earflaps – an essential article without which, he implied, no serious mountaineer was complete. I thought it made him look dangerously like Blashford-Snell, which was all the more worrying as he did not seem to mind.

Meanwhile Abdullah and Hassim were engaged in a bad-tempered discussion on the relative merits of forceful versus tractable camels for the task in hand. When eventually the five most suitable candidates were chosen, Dawn wasn't amongst them, but whether this was due to his being insufficiently forceful or insufficiently tractable was unclear. We led them up to a shallow terrace overlooking the camp for mounting, Wang Hai giving a last wave from below before diving into the warmth of his tent to await our return.

We followed the same route as the previous evening, climbing diagonally around the mountain flank, the glacier towering on our left. Abdullah led with Huang, George, myself and Tim following in single file behind. As usual Seyn pursued a roving commission.

We clawed our way steadily up the slope, the camels' bellies scraping outcrops on our right whilst hanging precariously over plunging scree on our left. It wasn't an encouraging view and, riding a few paces behind George, I could see his normal cheery disposition had deserted him. Twice, as his mount lurched and dipped, he leapt on to the uphill slope only to think better of it and clamber back on board shortly afterwards.

Our progress was agonisingly slow, the camels stumbling as they fought to cross the petrified rivers of rusty grey shale which erupted from the mountainside, their pads desperately searching for a foothold amongst the waiting blades. Step by step we inched upward whilst drop by drop the sun slowly emptied and gave way to an icy blue light shining from within the glacier itself.

Gradually we pulled out of the cleft between the glacier and the mountain and came level with the ice surface opposite. After striking the col where we had stopped the previous evening we slowly edged to the right along the contours high above the glacier pool. Then, zigzagging to lessen the pitch, we worked up to the point Abdullah had reached the night before.

A prospect both alluring and alarming opened out before us as we breasted the saddle. The ground fell away steeply to the shore of a frozen lake, its perfect surface framed by a chaos of rock and ice. On our left the glacier face, a tumbling mass of white and blue, hundreds of feet high, looked from this distance like a pile of children's building blocks. The lake itself stretched off ahead, its extent masked by a series of boulder-laden spurs plunging down from the mountain mass on our right, which created a succession of steep-sided bays on the northern shore. A steel-grey sky arched above and the air was still. For the moment, the barrier to further progress which the lake presented was forgotten. Who could fail to feel his heart lift when confronted by such a scene? It was a desolate and breathtaking sight and one that held us silently in its grasp.

The lake was completely missing from the Chinese map and its discovery seemed to confirm we were the first to try the route. Of course, it was possible that the expansion of the ice-field had dammed the meltwater outlet and created the lake since the map was published but a more likely explanation presented itself, as it was daily becoming more evident that the maps were relying increasingly on satellite imaging rather than land surveys. Our own satellite photos were very fuzzy in this area – largely due to ice glare – and it was therefore no surprise to find errors on maps based on them. It was this question which worried Huang. He seemed torn between pride at the discovery and embarrassment that the map was wrong. Seeing this, Tim and I stifled our initial enthusiasm for the lake. Frankly we also dreaded another of Huang's premature victory celebrations.

We dismounted here and, with one notable exception, foreswore riding for the rest of the day. Although walking along the slope was difficult it was by common consent infinitely preferable to lurching precariously ten feet above it. From now on the sole purpose of the camels was to prove they could cope with the country ahead, as pioneers for their comrades left in camp. It did cross my mind that we could simply try to complete the remainder of the expedition on foot, but even if the calculations of load versus distance could be reconciled, I was sure Huang would refuse to continue without camels.

An added result of the discovery of the lake was the realisation, again not unwelcome, that we had, for the foreseeable future, to find a route without benefit of map or satellite. We embarked on the now familiar polyglot discussion, accompanied by much pointing and grimacing. There seemed to be three alternatives. The first was to climb up the spur we were on and try to traverse the mountain at high level. The second was to try to edge around the contours to a saddle on the next spur. This would at least allow us to look into the second bay. The third alternative was to go down into the nearest bay and try to follow the lake shore around the spurs. The fourth unspoken alternative was, of course, to turn back. Having had the best part of a day to brood on the subject, this seemed to be Abdullah's preferred course of action. He sat down heavily on a boulder, surveyed the scene and gave a mournful twist of his moustache.

"Abdullah can go everywhere but the camels will die," was his response to each new suggestion. With his domed hat and puttees, his head cupped in his hands, today he looked more like Pierrot than Sancho Panza. Any further attempt to engage him in discussion of the route was met with a lugubrious silence, which he obviously thought was comment enough.

Our problem was that we simply didn't know how seriously to take his morbid predictions. So far the camels had proved to be sure-footed and calm but the routes ahead were of a different order of difficulty. The scree looked both steep and treacherous and I had visions of one slip sending the whole lot pitching down the slope in a single furry avalanche. On the other hand turning back wouldn't be an easy solution, as we certainly weren't going to abandon the expedition altogether. Our present route was in the nature of a short cut across the south-eastern corner of a range which both Littledale and Dutreuil de Rhins had found

more difficult than the Arka Tagh itself and if we turned back we
would still have to circumnavigate the whole range or cross it
further west as they had done. Either option would entail at least
eight days' extra travel and certainly exhaust our fodder. I knew
too that both Littledale's and de Rhins' routes had little to
recommend them. Littledale's account for 29th April 1895 ran;

> Having no guide, we took the most likely looking valley, and it
> ended in our camping near the summit of a pass in intense cold,
> where there was neither grass nor fuel. Having brought for an
> occasion like this some tins of Silver's self-boiling soup, personally
> we did pretty well. There was plenty of ice, but no fuel, so we
> could not melt it, and had a dry camp. A valuable horse died
> here. As he was travelling empty, I suppose the great elevation
> was the cause.

Two years earlier, Grenard had been even less encouraging.

> 26th September 1893
> We ascended by a steep slope, covered with several feet of snow,
> that which our leader mistakenly believed to be the chief chain of
> the system. On the other side, we camped, amid a confusion of
> blocks and of black schistose slabs, on the brim of a sort of dark
> funnel, overlooked by a chaos of fantastically shaped mountains
> which seemed, as it were, surprised to see us. At night we ex-
> perienced 30 degrees of cold and lost two horses. It was a fine
> start, an eloquent exordium "ex abrupto", but our resolve was
> taken, our determination fixed beforehand and our ears closed to
> all adverse argument.

Unfortunately for Abdullah we were in much the same frame
of mind regarding the present route. All our persuasive powers
were brought to bear on his hunched frame, Huang emphasising
the advantages of the route in conserving fodder whilst the rest of
us demonstrated by dint of dismissive gestures, how ridiculously
tame we considered the country ahead. I mentally prepared a list
of suitably shaming phases but luckily they weren't needed as he
was slowly cajoled into submission and agreed we should investigate the high level route.

We set off to scramble up to a knoll from where we hoped to have a clear view of the country ahead. We were now over 17,000 ft (5,180m), and the lack of oxygen began to take a serious toll for the first time. At this height the air pressure is almost exactly half that at sea level and, whilst at rest the effects were virtually unnoticeable, as soon as we started climbing each step became an ordeal and each breath a sucking gasp. I smiled with wry amusement at my plan, barely cold, to dispense with the camels' load-carrying services.

Tim took the climb in stages and rested whilst I preferred to slog slowly but surely up the slope, trying to build up a rhythm. It worked after a fashion. If I concentrated on beating the fire in my lungs, my legs proceeded at their own pace without conscious instructions. However, my growing satisfaction with this steady progress was quickly dissipated when George bounded past, maddeningly like a mountain goat. Now he was back on terra firma his enthusiasm had returned, along with his chipmunk smile.

"Why you go so slow?" he asked, with every sign of serious concern. He didn't understand my answer. Much as I liked George, I wasn't in a mood to appreciate this demonstration of his youthful exuberance. He obviously didn't realise how bad he was supposed to feel. I contented myself with the knowledge that he would regret it later. Maybe I even hoped he would regret it later.

In contrast, when we eventually reached the knoll, Abdullah and Huang could be seen half way down, having come to a dead stop.

Our hopes for a clear view to the west were disappointed, as it was still obscured by the top of the neighbouring spur. Teased by the prospect of being able to see over this obstruction, George and I decided to climb higher before returning. Tim decided to rest at the knoll.

Keeping our feet on the loose scree became increasingly difficult as the slope increased and it was a relief when we reached an outcrop which gave some tenuous handholds. I had left my over-mitts with the camels, and was wearing only a thin pair of inner gloves. Normally this was fine as the overmitts were very clumsy and the inners were adequate for daytime use, but they very quickly became torn as I used them on the sharp projections of the outcrop. At each attempted purchase the wafer thin leaves of rock cut into the flimsy material before finally pulling loose in a cascade of nascent scree. But the challenge was welcome and long overdue. Free of the camels, free of Huang, climbing high above the glacier, I felt happy at last. As we rose a second ice face came into view, capping the mountain above us and hanging precariously over our route.

Clambering over the edge of the outcrop we halted, panting, at about 18,100 ft (5,520m). Of course, I had omitted to relieve Tim of the altimeter when we left him on the knoll below. As we turned our backs to the mountain the whole of our southern horizon was filled with a vast fissured ice-field, stretching from the face far below to the distant skyline. Above it all the twin peaks of Ulugh Mustagh sailed majestically through a turbulent sea of clouds.

It was now clear that our route up to the saddle had followed a small tongue of this icefield which poked into the valley of the Ulugh Sou. Beyond it to the east other deeply crevassed glacier tongues cascaded into each succeeding valley. The scene lacked the serried verticality of the Himalaya but it would cede little in the way of sheer mountainous desolation to any area on earth. Even George, who until now had been heedless of sweeping vistas, seemed to be mildly impressed.

To the west we could now see over the top of our intended pass to where the icefield merged into the dim purple chain of the Arka Tagh, our ultimate objective. Unfortunately, we were no wiser about the details of the pass itself as the folds of the mountain flank still obscured the lower two routes. We now discounted the higher route. Even without the looming ice face it was obvious that the spur would be much too difficult for the camels.

Abdullah had evidently long since come to the same conclusion
and he could be seen below us clambering back from a reconnais-
sance to the second saddle. George and I slid downhill, scooping
up Tim and Huang on the way.

We fetched up with Abdullah half way down the spur and
squatted to consider the remaining routes. He still wasn't keen to
continue so once again he was subjected to the full force of our
encouragement. Huang, possibly fearing further loss of face,
seemed to be virtually ordering him to proceed, rapping out
staccato sentences whilst chopping down with his hand. Abdullah looked increasingly dejected with each chop. Not wishing to
add to his woes but determined to advance one way or the other,
I left them to it, merely asking in a sullen pause which route
Abdullah preferred. In the end he agreed, or at least we thought
he had agreed, to take the camels around the slope to the second
saddle.

As the camels were still below us, Abdullah set off to collect
them whilst we cut across to rendezvous on the slope. The flaw in
this arrangement became obvious when we looked back to see
him leading the camels down to the lakeshore in the first bay.
The unworthy thought crossed my mind that Abdullah was playing games with the Ferenghi Devils. Maybe he was just having
his revenge on Huang who was half way between the two parties
and seemed undecided which route he was taking. There was
nothing to do but to continue to the saddle and wait to see if they
reappeared on the lakeshore of the second bay.

Shafts of sunlight chased each other over the icefield as I
settled into an eyrie of russet scree high above the lake. The
frozen vision of icy grandeur before me was certainly awe-
inspiring but it held a greater power beyond even this. For here,
as in all wild places, I felt a deep sense of isolation and peace –
utterly alone and outside the physical world, yet perfectly reconciled to my place within it.

And within that world I allowed myself a brief moment of
satisfaction, even joy. The years of preparation, of permission

chasing and money raising, of turgid correspondence and even more turgid meetings, of alternate elation and despair – all these had been worthwhile. When I closed my eyes it seemed like a dream, but at this moment I could make the dream come true simply by opening them. The last shaft of sunlight receded and a cold wind blew up. I closed my eyes again and let my thoughts drift on...

Tim's whistle brought me back to consciousness and I rushed over to where he was perched on the headland between the bays. He had heard a loud commotion from below and thought there might have been an accident. We hurried down into the second bay only to find it was a false alarm. Both Abdullah and the camels were safe and well after successfully clambering along the lakeshore.

George had arrived before us and he reported that Huang had decided to stay in the first bay as he was tired. A wicked smile came to Abdullah's face as he gave his graphic opinion of Huang in a gesture that needed no translation. Even so, after my earlier strictures about safety I was only too aware how good mountaineering practice had suffered as we all pursued different routes out of sight of each other, and for a brief moment I thought of returning to Huang. But by now my resolve to drive on was too strong and the laudable thought was quickly suppressed.

We started off again scrambling over the rocks bordering the lake. At first led by Abdullah and then moving ahead of him we prepared a route for the camels. The scree had now changed character and looked more than ever like a devil's playground. Vertical outcrops of schist-like rock formed a jagged skyline along each spur whilst the bays between were filled with angular boulders which we pulled down and overturned to open a path. Abdullah was plainly less than happy but he kept going, coaxing and threatening the camels each time they pulled back until eventually they gave way and lurched forward again. Liberated from Huang's encouragement he seemed, at last, determined to press on. From time to time we halted to survey the prospect ahead but each time when we restarted he dutifully followed, the camels picking their way meticulously over the jagged shards. Several times they tried to bolt onto the lake surface and following Abdullah's lead we pelted them with stones to force them back up the mountainside. It wasn't humane but it was what we had come to expect and, most important of all, it was effective.

Seyn meanwhile frolicked in ecstasy on the ice. First ploughing nose down through the surface snow, then prancing with delight, she ranged far out onto the centre of the lake becoming an animated speck on the virgin surface.

We approached each headland with fresh hope for a long distance view only to have it dashed when yet another headland appeared beyond. Then came the task of guiding the camels round to the next bay, each headland becoming more difficult than the last as the shore steepened. After an hour's tortuous progress the lake first narrowed then ended completely in a narrow gulley a short distance from the ice face, forcing us to climb higher up the slope.

We stopped briefly and this time when we restarted Abdullah and the camels didn't follow. I had no complaints – Abdullah had done his best. He had kept going long after we had left Huang behind and for much of the route had led silently by example in preparing a path for the camels. But now he had obviously decided that both he and the camels had come far enough. Tim decided to stop here too. He was taking a long time to adjust to the altitude and had an even more languid air than usual. I put it down to the malign influence of the hat.

George and I set off westwards under a louring sky. The gulley below us continued parallel to the ice for a few hundred yards and then split into two ravines, one heading left towards the icefield and the other right towards the mountain. We turned up the slope to reach a section of the right-hand ravine which was shallow enough to cross. Squalls of snow spiralled down as we climbed and by the time we reached the ravine proper, the jagged landscape around us was being gentled by an icy veil. We crossed to the far side and scrambled up a rocky projection, the wind slowly mounting in force as we approached the skyline.

Here, stung by the snow, we again strained our eyes to the west. Between flurries we could dimly see what seemed to be a watershed joining the icefield to the mountain. Our route lay over this watershed but it was impossible to judge the severity of the near slopes. And what lay beyond remained a mystery. Even if the watershed really was the summit of the pass, we could still find the far slopes impossible to descend. In any case it was an open question whether the camels would be able to reach our present position.

It was frustrating. Each new horizon was surmounted by another, yet we couldn't go on forever. It was already five hours since we had started from Glacier Camp. Huang was somewhere back in the first bay (or so I thought), Tim and Abdullah were specks in the gloom beneath us and I was becoming increasingly weary. Slowly but surely the cold, altitude and effort were exacting their price in fatigue.

George showed no outward sign of feeling the same but his comments on the route were uncharacteristically monosyllabic. What did he think of the country ahead, I shouted. Hard, he thought. Hard but possible? Possible he thought. So we would tell Huang that we could come this way with the camels? Yes, agreed George. Should we return now? Yes.

We retraced our steps in the gathering blizzard, feet slithering over the iced slabs, ankles gambling with a compound fracture. We were slower now and the ground was transformed to an unknown landscape. I had lost sight of Tim and the others and was beginning to think we had missed them when they loomed, statue-like, out of the murk, their coats caked with snow. I nearly fell over Seyn who was once again successfully imitating a snowball. Tim was obviously irritated by our longer-than-expected absence but he sensibly restrained his wrath and instead helped to dislodge ice from my eyebrows and beard. They had managed to turn the camels round, a considerable feat on the sloping scree, and we started back immediately.

We had been going about twenty minutes when suddenly an ethereal form appeared drifting over the lake. It was Huang, still in this life and walking over the frozen surface. After sitting in the first bay for a while, he had decided to avoid the agony of the route by simply taking to the ice. The rest of us had tacitly avoided this until now, partly because we weren't confident that the ice would hold us, but also because it would probably encourage the camels to follow. Since the ice was as thick as a man's thigh, we were probably being ridiculously conservative about our own safety, but the camels were another matter. An unladen Bactrian camel weighs over half a ton and if we lost any now Abdullah would certainly refuse to go further.

We set off through the storm with Huang, the humans occasionally creeping on to the ice when the camels weren't looking. But progress was becoming impossible. Skidding over the snow-covered boulders, the camels became drunken spiders, their legs splaying out in a desperate attempt to stay upright. Eventually, when we came to the worst section, Abdullah led them out onto the lake. We held our collective breath but the surface held and from now on we took them onto the ice increasingly often. It was a chance we had to take; we could neither make progress along the mountainside nor stop where we were with the camels in such a skittish mood. The camels simply voted with their feet and made a break for the ice whenever the occasion offered. We kept close into the shore although even this presented a dilemma as the ice was probably thinnest here – but to move further out would remove all chance of rescue in case of collapse.

Once on the ice, freed from the clatter of dislodged stones, our footfalls muffled by the thickening snow, the silence was total. Each of us was in his own dense white world, within sight of other dim silhouettes but far enough away, we hoped, to reduce the risk of breaking through the ice. A single report reverberated through the gloom but no crack appeared and we forged on.

After a while I moved out on to the ice to take a photo of the camels and Abdullah as they came round a rocky headland. As I focused through the view finder, Number Three simply disappeared. It had broken through the ice and instantly submerged in the water below. I dropped the camera and rushed to where Abdullah was tugging at the lead camel's halter.

By the time I reached him Number Three had surfaced and was threshing around in terror, breaking the surrounding ice. The two rear camels tried to pull back but couldn't as they were tied to Number Three. The ice collapsed beneath them and they slid forward into the churning pool. Abdullah had managed to pull the lead camel on to the rocks but Number Two was still half submerged, bellowing and pawing panic stricken at the shore to avoid being pulled back into the melee. I grabbed the leader and shouted to Abdullah to cut the rope and concentrate on Number Two while I pulled the leader up the slope to safety.

Surrounded by a roaring cacophony I noticed Tim and the others for the first time, running back towards us over the scree. But even as I raised my head they froze, hands on knees, gulping for air. The fifty-yard dash had simply exhausted their stores of oxygen. Gasping, they came on, and together we hauled on the ropes and harangued the camels in the seething tumult below.

With its head beneath the surface, Number Three appeared to have foundered completely, its dead weight defeating camels fore and aft as they strove to find their feet in the shelving margin and pull on to the shore. Then, suddenly, it revived, its neck rearing into the air and lashing at the surrounding ice, its body contorting in an effort to turn towards the land. George dropped the rope, unsheathed his knife and lunged towards its neck, missing as it pulled away. Ignoring our shouts, he dodged between waves of foam and lunged again, his motive finally clear as he held aloft his bag, cut loose from the submerged saddle.

The contest had to be resolved one way or the other and as the camels tired, the turmoil subsided. First Number Two, then the back markers were coaxed and hauled one by one on to the shore. As we lay shattered on the scree, even Number Three stood petrified beside us, its coat instantly turned to a hard iced shield. No bones were broken but it was losing blood slowly from a gash on the left foreleg. Abdullah signed that the injury was of no consequence, yet I was uncomfortably aware that his predictions of camels dying had come perilously close to being fulfilled. In the process I had completely lost track of time. The whole episode had probably taken less than ten minutes but every second was still in crisp focus and it felt like hours had elapsed since I first raised the camera.

Looking at Abdullah's haggard, snow-plastered face, I realised I must present an equally ghostly aspect. We had better press on. We started around the headland, keeping the camels well up the slope. As before, it was hard work but the blizzard had abated slightly and the shore was less steep than it had been further west. We were making faster progress now and the worst of our problems seemed to be over.

Eventually, we arrived in the first bay at the point where Abdullah had joined the shore. Above us was the saddle where we had dismounted a lifetime ago. A faint brown line threaded down, betraying Abdullah's route to the lake. The prospect of climbing up to the saddle didn't appeal and we looked for alternatives. Maybe there was a better route which would also serve if we brought over laden camels in the coming days. If we followed the shore there might be an easier passage along the glacier edge. On the other hand, it might be impassable. Abdullah and Huang preferred to go over the saddle with the camels but we agreed that the rest of us should try the shore route. We fixed a rendezvous on the far side of the saddle and set off our different ways again. It was the wrong decision, but laziness and fatigue are a potent brew.

Soon after, we rounded the final headland and were confronted by an irresistible force meeting its immovable object. At the lake end the glacier was ploughing into the base of the mountain spur, throwing up car-sized boulders of ice and rock at the junction. Although the actual movement was imperceptible, it was as if we had turned the headland just in time to see the results of a high-speed collision. This barrier had no doubt created the lake by damming the outlet, but at what time in the past it had first happened we had no idea.

We clambered over the calving slabs and slid down into a small bay enclosed between mountain and glacier. Watermarks etched into the scree showed that the frozen pool trapped against the glacier had once reached higher levels. After skirting the pool we climbed over a low col and found ourselves on a shoulder of the main spur overlooking the rendezvous point. On balance, this route had been easier than the saddle but the boulder-strewn sections would be too hard for the camels.

The last flurries of snow disappeared over the glacier as we sat down to await the others. The rest of the route would be downhill and we looked forward to reaching Glacier Camp within the hour.

But it was not to be. After a while Abdullah appeared on the saddle leading the camels. But Huang was nowhere to be seen. We watched Abdullah descend, the camels strung out along the scree on the far side of the valley. From our vantage point they looked as if they were glued to the opposite face of the mountain.

There was a long wait before Huang finally appeared, moving very slowly and resting every fifty yards. He looked spent. Abdullah meanwhile ploughed on half a mile ahead. We followed Huang's distant drama in silence. I knew we had been wrong to split into two parties again – it might yet have serious results.

As we watched, Huang's progress became even slower, the period between rests shorter and shorter. It was clear he was totally exhausted and I was tempted to pitch the tent and brew up a hot drink, at a stroke saving his life and vindicating our preparations. But to do this we would have to arrest Abdullah's headlong flight along the opposite slope.

Then a simpler solution presented itself. But we would still have to halt Abdullah. Unfortunately, he was out of earshot across a wide scree-covered valley. Tim and I were dog tired and

I was sure if we tried to get over to him, he would be a long way down the valley before we caught him. George, by contrast, still showed irritating signs of life. I tentatively suggested that Huang needed help or he wouldn't survive. Could George get over to Abdullah and tell him to stop and put Huang on a camel? George said Huang was fine, and anyway he wasn't George's responsibility. There was certainly no love lost between the two of them, as we had seen on the approach, and my best attempts to call on George's sympathy met an implacable resolve to let Huang find his own salvation.

I saw no alternative and decided on one last desperate throw. In the most authoritative voice I could muster, I ordered George to cross over to Abdullah. Conditioned by twenty-seven years' obedience to authority, he dutifully obeyed, which thankfully avoided the consideration that I had no right to give the order in the first place. He started a small avalanche as he descended and crossed the valley bottom to the opposite slope. Climbing diagonally to intercept Abdullah, he started at a run and gradually slowed as he gained height.

The plan worked. The two waited for Huang to reach them and loaded him on to Number Two. We roused ourselves from our role as spectators and headed downhill to meet at the col above Glacier Camp. All three of us avoided mention of this episode, for our different reasons, when later discussing the day's happenings. I was none too proud of splitting the party again at the lake, Huang obviously felt a great loss of face and George presumably didn't want to admit it had taken a direct order for him to go to his leader's aid.

It was a very subdued party which stumbled into camp at 7.30 that night. Even George's cheery disposition had deserted him. His climb up to Abdullah had finally brought him to the same stage of exhaustion as the rest of us, an unlooked-for bonus of the affair. By now I was becoming prone to unworthy thoughts such as this. Huang followed behind slumped sack-like on his camel, his broken glasses hanging by the string from one ear. The exception to the general prostration was Seyn whose stamina put us all to shame. She had romped ahead, tail wagging, down the final slopes and was already making short work of a lamb bone.

It took several requests before those left in camp would brew up a hot drink to revive us but at least Wang Hai, seeing how slow we were, helped to pitch the tent. Tim's offer to rub down the frozen camel was met with laughter by Abdullah. Of course, it would be fine. There was no need. What a ridiculous suggestion. And in truth he was right, all five camels completing the expedition without any sign of ill effect from their sub-zero plunge.

The hot drink revived us all and even Huang raised a smile when I poked my head into his tent.

"Tonight eat and sleep, tomorrow rest and talk," I ventured.

"OK, Williamo," he agreed.

Later, slurping down warm tinned pears, Tim and I mulled over the day's events.

One thing was certain, neither George nor Abdullah had any great love for Huang and were glad when they were rid of him. I felt much the same. Often, I found myself consciously trying to summon up enough Sino-British friendship to overcome my outrage at the latest exposure of his deviousness. At other times, when he was arguing with the other Chinese I had a residual feeling that the British Leader should be supporting his position, however stupid. But my reservoir of duty was unequal to the task and by now I could do little better than endure him. Even my sympathy for his plight at the saddle had been tempered by a dawning awareness that he was physically unfit for such an expedition. Today was the first day we had spent largely on foot due to the difficulty of the terrain. Whichever route we took there would be much more of this from now on. How would Huang cope? Like the Beijing jeep, he was becoming more of a liability than an asset.

For me it had been one of the hardest but most exhilarating days of my life. However, the problem of the pass remained to be solved. I was sure it was worth another try and George and Tim seemed to be of the same mind. The question was, would Huang and Abdullah agree?

"I'm sure they'll want to go back now," was the closing entry in my diary.

That night, as our restless beasts bellowed in the resurgent blizzard, I slipped in and out of consciousness, my early dreams of panic-stricken camels fading imperceptibly into the tangled chaos of Picasso's *Geurnica*.

CHAPTER 8

Arka Tagh

By the next morning Huang had recovered in both body and soul and was willing to give the pass another try. But we were still faced with a more practical worry – our rapidly shrinking stock of fodder. Despite all our exhortations Abdullah and Hassim had continued to feed the animals like there was no tomorrow with the result that we were down to five days' supplies. Time was now the major problem and crossing the pass ever more critical. Tim and I would have a hell of a job convincing the others to try a second route if the pass did prove impossible. We briefly considered leaving part of the team at Glacier Camp with a dump of provisions and most of the camels, whilst a smaller party pressed on to gain the Kara Muran. This would allow us to travel more quickly – and I secretly hoped that Huang would opt to lead the rearguard. But he wouldn't take the hint and in the end it was decided we would all go, leaving a depot at Glacier Camp and travelling as lightly as possible.

The rest of the day was free. According to our original plan this was the sort of day we should have spent rummaging around in the surrounding mountains but we were too tired and spent the time recuperating, reading and snoozing, as indeed we did virtually every day we weren't on the march. I later regretted some of the wasted opportunities but life was demanding enough as it was and we needed the break.

The weather was calmer now. Snow and sun alternated, first covering the grey surface in a thick carpet of white then melting it into the thirsty ground below. The scree showed an unquenchable appetite and even a heavy fall of snow soon disappeared. Freed from their bonds the camels mooched around camp like ghosts at the feast, their whitened flanks holding snow long after the surrounding ground had cleared.

Later I walked along the glacier face, the whole fissured edifice glinting and shimmering in the evening light like the setting for a Nordic Saga. Here too there was life. I watched fascinated as an orange butterfly bobbed and weaved towards the setting sun. Then my eye was caught by a sudden movement and I wheeled round to see a hare clambering by invisible ledges up the near vertical ice into a hanging chasm twenty or thirty feet above the valley floor.

There was a clear sky and a brilliant sun as we started towards the pass for the third time the next morning – and this time it lasted for most of the day. The fine weather made a tremendous difference and where before we had been enveloped in blinding snow today there was only the inviting prospect of a sunny promenade. We reached the lake without mishap and started along the shore. Then without warning the camels pulled out on to the ice and refused all efforts to force them back. Luckily the ice had strengthened and although the camels were more heavily laden than before, the surface held. The caravan presented a bizarre yet magnificent sight as it stretched out over the shining surface, silhouetted against the sharp triangular spurs and cobalt blue sky.

Our tracks of two days before had been covered and replaced by the recent spoor of a fox, half the length of Seyn. And even as I stooped to measure them, another surprise, a small black spider scuttled past heading for the white infinity beyond.

By taking a different line and zigzagging through a maze of boulders we managed to haul the camels up to the watershed George and I had dimly glimpsed two days before. The rest of us were on foot but Huang stayed in the saddle throughout – on balance probably a good idea and in everyone's interests. As I had feared, the watershed was a false summit but at least the true summit was visible at the far end of a shallow rise. By now Tim had got his second wind and was determined to arrive somewhere first so he and George entered into a discreet but determined race for the summit. Approaching from opposing flanks and studiously ignoring each other's progress they eventually breasted the pass side by side – but as Tim later put it, "Being a head taller, I saw first that success was possible".

When everyone had finally arrived Huang took the usual round of "Victory" photographs – one of the most trying features of the whole expedition. Wang Hai laughed at a quiet aside of Abdullah's.

"He says Chinese not get here without British to push them." I took it as a heartfeit compliment, but wasn't totally oblivious of the irony, considering my recent plans to leave Huang at Glacier Camp.

The upper basin of the Kara Muran lay spread before us, a sunlit but barren panorama of rock and ice. On our left the ice-field continued westward before finally running out into the heavily eroded slopes of the Arka Tagh. Twenty miles to the west a single precocious peak climbed higher than its neighbours, its upper slopes plastered with permanent snow. A parallel range of snow-capped peaks enclosed the valley on the north whilst below us an easy slope led down to the valley floor.

We rested at the pass. The summit itself was at 17,585 ft (5,360m). Huang suggested we name the pass and the lake. At first we proposed Lake Abdullah as he had been first to see it but Huang rejected this as Abdullah was "not a full member of the expedition". I then declined Lake Holgate and we eventually settled on Philippa Kol (Kol meaning Lake) in honour of my girlfriend. It was a modest little lake, probably less than two miles long, but she later professed herself perfectly satisfied. The pass was similarly named Patricia Davan in honour of Tim's girlfriend. I'm sure Lake Huang and Sino-British Friendship Pass would have been more diplomatic but I was past caring for such niceties. In any case, we had few illusions that the names would be incorporated on to future Chinese maps – and even these fragile hopes were to disappear as our relations with Huang worsened further.

We slowly picked our way down the western slopes into the basin below. By now I saw Hassim as the more humane of the two camel drivers and this was reinforced when we came to a thin trickle of ice-covered water, the headwaters of the Kara Muran. Pausing to break the ice he let his camels drink in turn while Abdullah forced his string onward. My convictions lasted for two hours until Hassim's camel halted and couched. He flayed its muzzle mercilessly for five minutes until it rose again and continued. Possibly he was being cruel to be kind as any beast abandoned here would have precious little chance of survival.   .

The end of the icefield when it came was a jagged line against the deeply incised slopes of the Arka Tagh which here rose in layer upon layer to the southern horizon. We tried with scant success to relate this complex maze of fans and screes to either the map or the satellite photos. As we continued westward the valley widened and the scree gave way to the familiar gravel terraces. A single wagtail flitted between the only vegetation, isolated clumps of hard, pink-flowered moss.

We kept on for ten miles after we had left the icefield and camped at the mouth of a tributary we hoped led to the Kara Muran Davan. This camp, Camp 10, was our highest at 17,045 ft (5,195m). Here we rejoined the routes of Dutreuil de Rhins and Littledale for the last time. It was a timely reunion for the expedition was often swelled by the ghosts of our predecessors. Many times on the march I had seen the shades of the Littledales riding side by side or heard the echoes of Dutreuil de Rhins' peremptory commands ringing out across the valley. Later Hassim found a rusty iron bowl projecting from the terrace not far from camp and we spent many fruitless hours in speculation whether it had been left by Littledale or a twentieth century Chinese surveyor.

Dutreuil de Rhins and Littledale had approached our present position from the west after completing difficult mountain passages. These had proved so trying that both had been deceived into believing the previous chain to be the Arka Tagh and had been dismayed to be confronted by a further range. Littledale, being further west, had then wasted ten frustrating days searching for a suitable pass before coming on the tributary. Hedin had also briefly joined the route and we were united at last for the final climb to the Tibetan Plateau.

That night we tried cooking the dehydrated food for the first time. Abdullah and Hassim kept to the lamb ostensibly on religious grounds but really, I think, because they didn't trust the new stuff. Otherwise the main meals were popular enough but only Seyn appreciated the deserts. She could be seen later that night waddling between the camels replete with six helpings of apple and custard mash.

George woke us early the next morning with the news that Abdullah was ill. He lay in his tent complaining of serious pains in his neck. I gave him a couple of Paracetamol which he retched up, so I tried Soluble Aspirin. Later he seemed worse. He complained almost incoherently of headache and his legs had swollen. I left him with Hassim while I went to look up my medical notes.

The neck pains, confusion and headache were classic symptoms of Cerebral Oedema in which excess fluid collects in the brain. It was a serious condition and one which could quickly be fatal. The swelling in the legs, or Peripheral Oedema wasn't in itself life threatening but it tended to confirm the other diagnosis. The UIAA notes went on; "It cannot be stated frequently enough that the most efficacious treatment is to descend rapidly to a lower altitude."

It was impossible. In our present position, all routes led upwards, with the exception of a barely perceptible fall to the west along the Kara Muran. It would take the best part of a week travelling away from our supply dumps to descend the required 1,500 ft in that direction. And we were almost three weeks from the nearest telephone and radio – not that contact with the outside world would be any help. Rapid descent would still be impossible and there was no known drug which reliably cured the condition. My notes suggested that rest and a course of Diamox (acetazolamide) might just possibly work in early Cerebral Oedema so I decided to try it.

It was ironic that Abdullah, who lived at 10,000 ft (3,000m) should be affected more than the rest of us – but Cerebral Oedema seems to be no respecter of simple rules when it chooses its victims. Altitude had obviously been a factor in Huang's exhaustion of three days before but this apart the rest of us were encountering few serious problems. Like everyone else I suffered from swollen and cracked lips, and the cuts on my hands refused to heal but this was to be expected and I now felt much more relaxed about my own health.

Partly this was due to a calmer assessment of the risks involved but there was too my growing acceptance of those remaining risks. Resigned to the remoteness of medical help, removed from familiar pressures, familiar worries and the clutter of familiar thoughts, I faced the prospect of death with greater equanimity than ever before or since. Much as I wanted to live, where better to be overtaken by the inescapable?

Abdullah slept most of the day, groaning occasionally and rousing only to take some tea and Diamox. I had grown to like both him and Hassim over the previous weeks as they were both taciturn but friendly and got on with the task in hand. Abdullah did sometimes like to be more showy and had the domed hat and suede boots to carry it off. He obviously regarded himself as the equal of Huang and myself and was quite willing to argue if necessary – although luckily this wasn't too frequently.

His sudden illness presented us with a serious dilemma. We had already stayed at Camp 10 an extra day, we had the bare minimum of fuel and fodder, and time was pressing. To make matters worse Abdullah certainly couldn't be taken any higher – the Kara Muran Davan was out of the question. It was implicit that his safety came first but it's hard to describe the depth of our frustration at the prospect of being denied the pass. Known country as it was, the Kara Muran Davan had steadily assumed a symbolic position in our ambitions.

We harried the problem from all sides in between checking Abdullah's condition and eventually decided to leave him with a minder and attempt to reach the pass and return in a single day. The next question was who would stay with him. Tim generously volunteered but I insisted we draw lots and in the end we postponed a decision until we could see the patient's state the following morning.

This dawned cold and clear to reveal Abdullah partly recovered and, I judged, well enough to leave alone. He tied Seyn to keep him company.

This was Hassim's chance for modest fame in Bash Malghun although it had no noticeable effect on his customary phlegm. So far he had remained virtually monosyllabic throughout, our conversations being made up of gestures and grunts. But he had proved reliable and we had warmed to him. His relative poverty was evident and his wardrobe was considerably smaller than Abdullah's, comprising a series of flimsy cotton jackets, luckily supplemented by our contribution of a sheepskin greatcoat. This was topped by a sheepskin cap which he rarely removed and we had been taken aback a week into the expedition when he doffed it for his morning ablutions to reveal a perfectly bald pate beneath.

We started early up the wide valley to the south. We were still far from sure that this was the route Dutreuil de Rhins, Littledale and Hedin had taken but as the day progressed it seemed increasingly likely.

Soon after starting we startled an antelope and fawn who raced off to the west. Then Seyn arrived, the remains of her neatly bitten leash hanging from her neck. Her loyalty to Abdullah, such as it was, couldn't rival the thrill of the trail.

The valley gradually narrowed and we crossed and recrossed the stream, which was heavily iced with crystal patterns etched into the surface. Where it was against the rock face it had melted with reflected heat whilst elsewhere the water could be seen running below the ice. Sometimes the camels broke through with the characteristic "Crumph".

Presently the main valley slid round to the east and we followed the stream as it turned into a side ravine leading south. Now the upper sunlit slopes were obscured by lower craggy outcrops sheltering isolated snowdrifts. A small orange-tailed bird flashed in and out of the sun above our heads. Higher still an eagle slipped the wind and followed our progress. The ravine sides closed further until we were climbing up a rocky defile, the clatter of dislodged stones echoing back from the walls. The floor twisted back and forth, forking into a tangled labyrinth of ramps and boulders. Pausing to discuss each new choice, we held as closely as possible to the south.

This was the final test and one which Hedin had nearly failed. Relying upon the faulty memory of Hamdan Bai, one of Littledale's men, he had been led astray up one of these forks to the north-east, only later regaining his southerly route.

For the moment I was fairly confident we were close to the lines taken by Dutreuil de Rhins and Littledale but our own choice of route was far from unanimous and tension mounted as the pass remained elusive. Then, just as doubt threatened to triumph, the floor of the defile dried and steepened. We clambered up a stony ramp and suddenly we were on the crest of the Arka Tagh. At last I looked down from the Kara Muran Davan over the Plateau of Tibet.

Even this long awaited consummation couldn't compete with that first superb revelation of lake, rock and ice at the saddle above Glacier Camp but I did have an intense feeling of contentment and completion. For a few moments I was oblivious to the surrounding commotion as I took in the barren but deeply satisfying sight before me.

The southern slopes of the range were less incised than the northern and led down between snow-streaked outliers to the undulating plain below. The ground was purple-brown and naked and even the intense midday sun couldn't lessen its utter desolation. To the south-south-east at the centre of the plain lay the thin green-white line of Grenard's Lac des Corbeaux (Raven Lake). Directly south two conical hills were topped by black tuff summits. Otherwise the surface ran with little relief forty miles to the crisp blue outline of the Kokoshili Mountains.

I was awoken from my reverie by Huang acting as Master of Ceremonies in a barrage of staged photographs and Victory salutes. He never did understand my quiet pleasure on these occasions and here at the culmination of the whole expedition he was even more baffled. I did mean to shake Tim's hand but forgot and it had to wait until Hong Kong. He, meanwhile, showed no desire to be distracted from his first sight of Tibet.

Hassim also took the proceedings quietly as, swathed in his full length sheepskin he leant on the neck of his couched camel and scanned the southern horizon. Catching my eye he gave a brief nod of acknowledgement and murmured "Yahxi" (Good).

"Yahxi," I agreed.

The pass at 18,010 ft (5,490m) was little lower than the surrounding mountains. After the official group photographs we dispersed and spent an hour or so descending a few hundred yards into Tibet and investigating the rock formations. So far George had been the only one of the Chinese who had taken his scientific duties seriously, collecting geological samples and making field notes throughout the expedition. We had originally been told that the government prohibited the collection of botanical, entomological and geological specimens by foreigners. But by now it was clear that Huang either didn't know or didn't care about the ruling and I had belatedly joined George in his activities.

My samples were later analysed by Mike Searle of Oxford University. The main question they touched on was the longstanding debate about the origin of the north Tibetan plateau. One theory suggested that the northern movement of the Indian subcontinent was thrusting below Central Asia, whilst the second theory suggested it was compressing Central Asia. Peter Molnar, a geologist in the 1985 expedition, had discovered outcrops of young granites on the far side of Ulugh Mustagh which, together with other features, tended to resolve the debate in favour of compression melting and thickening the earth's crust. Searle had hoped that we would provide further confirmation of this to the west of Ulugh Mustagh, preferably in the form of granite samples, and our limestones, sandstones and schists were, I'm afraid, a great disappointment to him.

Later, waiting for the others to return I lay on the southern slopes following in my mind's eye the travails of our predecessors as they struggled on towards Lhasa.

CHAPTER 9

The Silver Collar

Dutreuil de Rhins' and Grenard's progress, already tortuous, was now further hampered by the slow disintegration of their caravan. For five weeks they struggled across the windswept plateau, unable to prevent the rising death toll amongst their animals or the progressive demoralisation of their men. Then on 9th November 1893 they were confronted by the first of many Tibetan envoys. He pleaded with them to return northward, saying he would be beheaded if his mission was unsuccessful. This was a common stratagem but not one to influence Dutreuil de Rhins who pressed on for a further three weeks until halted by exhaustion at Zamna near the Nam Cho. The fate of the envoy is not recorded.

At Zamna, with their provisions finished and over half their animals dead they were soon surrounded by an armed Tibetan guard. The two explorers now entered into negotiations with a succession of increasingly senior envoys, negotiations which were to drag on for fifty days as conditions in the camp steadily deteriorated. All but two of the remaining animals died, many being attacked whilst they lay alive but unable to resist.

"The neighbourhood of the camp became a charnel house," wrote Grenard, "Great crows settled on their backs and drove the hard horn of their beaks into their open sores, with the quiet satisfaction of an honest burgess sitting down to his dinner."

Dutreuil de Rhins, already ill, began to have periodic blackouts and his men gradually defected until forced to return by the Tibetans. Eventually there was no alternative but to accept the Tibetans' offers of provisions and transport, turn aside from Lhasa and head eastwards.

By the summer they had reached Tumbumdo in north-eastern

Tibet, having buried their interpreter Yunus en route. Here two horses disappeared and two local horses were seized as security for their return. But Dutreuil de Rhins, a former naval officer variously described as "a stickler for discipline" and "plain spoken" had fatally miscalculated the Tibetan response. The villagers attacked, seriously wounding him and forcing the rest of the party to flee in confusion. Rassul Galwan recorded an account of Dutreuil de Rhins' end by one of the camel drivers.

> And Mohammed Isa return. Said the sahib not had died. After two days the Tanguts tied his hands with rope and threw him into the river. There swam the sahib. Then the Tanguts put a stone on his head. Then he died in that.

It took Grenard a further six months to reach Beijing and by the time he made it back to France, Littledale was already en route.

One of Littledale's first actions on crossing the Kara Muran Davan was to measure the height of Ulugh Mustagh at 25,339 ft (7,723m), a height widely used for the following century, rather unfairly passing over surveys by his predecessors.

Przhevalsky had probably been the first westerner to see the peak, reporting "a lofty, sharply defined peak" in the distance south-west of his 1884 route. He couldn't measure the height but four years later Pevtsov was more fortunate, arriving at a figure of 23,700 ft (7,224m). In 1893 Dutreuil de Rhins measured the height at 24,147 ft (7,360m). A century later the Sino-American expedition, using a barrage of electronic devices arrived at 22,916 ft (6,985m). As this is almost certainly accurate to within 23 ft (7m) it suggests that both Pevtsov and Dutreuil de Rhins were not only earlier but also more accurate than Littledale. None of which detracts from his outstanding achievement, particularly in view of our own experience. We were correcting our barometric altimeter at those positions on the Chinese maps we thought were ground surveyed. The result was an accumulated correction of 778 ft (237m) equal to a variation in pressure at sea level of 25mb. This is perfectly normal but seeing its implications in practice was an eye opener.

Once on the Tibetan Plateau, Littledale discharged the supplementary men he had engaged at Charchan and they returned with 130 of the animals, their task now complete. Hearing that Mula Shah, one of those who had been paid to continue, intended to defect with the Charchan men he took the precaution of handcuffing him for a few days. Such incidents appear rarely in Littledale's explorations and Younghusband later wrote, with unintended irony;

> Littledale was graced with the happy knack of getting on with all kinds and all sorts of people and of carrying them along with him.

The key to this success is suggested by Rassul Galwan who describes Littledale lending his riding pony to his servants while he walked beside them. By all accounts there seems to be little doubt that both Littledale and his wife had more modest and placid temperaments than their contemporaries, notwithstanding a necessary streak of determination. However neither modesty nor determination were of use as the expedition met the familiar litany of disaster.

> Owing to the high altitude, scarcity of food, and cold, our animals began to die off at an appalling rate.... Not a day passed but several animals had to be shot or abandoned, (wrote Littledale. He also decided to jettison all inessentials),
>
> ... clothes, camp furniture and natural history specimens, horse shoes, even the very bindings of books which were essential, were ruthlessly abandoned. Our men, seeing new clothes thus thrown away wished to exchange their own rags for them; we told them they might take what they liked, but if anyone took a coat, for instance, he must leave his own in exchange. It was, perhaps, a little difficult to arrange an exact equivalent for some ladies' garments.

The party was eventually halted at the Goring La, 48 miles from Lhasa. As usual the first entreaty was by an emissary fearful for his own neck, this being soon followed by a series of more peremptory commands. They still had sufficient food to withstand a two month siege, but in the end it was Mrs Littledale's deteriorating health which caused Littledale to submit and head for Ladak. By now his wife had to be carried on a litter but she later made a complete recovery. The expedition's animals were less fortunate and of the 120 that had come through from Charchan and a further 50 purchased from the Tibetans, only eight reached Srnigar.

All Littledale's specimens except his dried plants were shipwrecked on the return journey but both he and his wife returned safely to a long life of rural contentment. Their nephew, William Fletcher, went on to fight in the Boer and First World Wars, dying as a result of being gassed. Tanny, the fox terrier, was made a Fellow of the Royal Geographical Society, which also voted him a silver collar in recognition of his exploits.

The question may be asked, "Having come so far why didn't we too press on towards Lhasa?" The immediate answer is that we had not planned to do so – and therefore had neither permission nor sufficient supplies. But there is also a simpler reason. For whilst I had become fascinated by Littledale and the others during those frustrating years when the Chinese had refused permission for my own journey, the historical parallels were still secondary to my joy in reaching and exploring the Arka Tagh themselves.

For the present we were in better shape than our predecessors – Littledale had lost eight animals on this single day's climb to the Kara Muran Davan – and we had every reason to believe our luck would hold.

CHAPTER 10

Retreat

"Tugeh oldi," announced Hassim.

"Luotuo si," translated Huang.

"Camel died," translated George in turn. All of which was superfluous as *Tugeh oldi* was one of my few Turki phrases and failing that I could hardly miss the very obvious bulk of a dead camel outside the tent door.

It was only an hour since we had completed an uneventful descent from the Kara Muran Davan but the dead camel was one of those we had left behind in camp. It was moreover one of the biggest and strongest of our beasts. Hassim said it had been fine earlier but had then just collapsed. It lay on its side, its neck strangely rubbery, its eyes gazing sightlessly towards the mountains, as a trickle of yellow fluid oozed from the corner of its mouth on to the frozen ground. Its comrades circled the body, puzzled and restive.

As evening approached a solitary raven came stealing from the Arka Tagh and circled above the corpse. Then at sunset the valley head cleared and the lifeless form was silhouetted against the double white triangle of Ulugh Mustagh whilst above the sky blazed with a glowing requiem of muave and purple.

Almost certainly it had died of a heart attack due to the altitude and cold. Although still warm during the early afternoon, the evening temperatures were now bitter. The previous night the thermometer had fallen to 0°F (−17.5°C) but there was also a constant biting wind and I calculated that the wind-chill factor made the effective temperature closer to −40°F (−40°c). Abdullah had started using his suede boots, Hassim had donned the felt equivalent and we were becoming seriously worried abut Wang Hai who was constantly complaining of cold feet. We had already given him and the others all our spare socks but there was a limit to the number of pairs his flimsy boots would hold.

"At least Abdullah now has a big enough weight for tethering the camels," quipped Tim as we closed the tent for the night. Even so we were shocked to find just that on opening the flap the next morning. A ring of doleful camels was tethered to the legs and neck of their defunct companion. The pool of body fluid had frothed up like soap suds during the night and was blowing in delicate whisps across the valley floor.

Abdullah showed every sign of having made a complete recovery but we continued to give him Diamox to avoid any recurrence of his condition as we were now obliged to climb back over the pass to Glacier Camp. It was a risk, but an unavoidable one.

We set out early towards the ice-field. We were all subdued and became even more so a few hours later when we came to the valley head. Faced with the steepening slope one of the two most frail camels stopped dead then sat down. Hassim tried to force it on but relatively mildly compared with his previous efforts. He obviously had little hope of its continuing. Then he and Abdullah took off its saddle and pulled out its noseplug. Hassim made one last despairing effort and managed to force it to its feet. It stood unsteadily as we started up the slope but didn't follow, a lonely figure watching us diminish into the distance. Hassim was upset for a long time afterwards and kept kneeling on his saddle to look back as his beast slowly disappeared. Its chances of survival were negligible.

When we reached the ice-field we took a new line up to the pass. Here the scree was streaked with a regular pattern of drainage channels about three metres apart – all part of nature's strange self regulation achieved without the intervention of human hand.

We dismounted at the pass with a superb view of Ulugh Mustagh climbing above the ice-field. We also had a clear view of the ice-field on top of the mountains to the north. After sliding down to the lake our camels once again insisted on taking to the ice. By now it must have been much thicker than before as the temperature was a good deal lower. At least, we had no problems.

We arrived at Glacier camp in mid afternoon and Tim seeing this as his last chance roped me in, literally, for an ascent of the glacier face. Luckily my role was simply to belay Tim as he started hesitantly up the vertical face. He did three short pitches, front pointing with his crampons and two ice-axes and putting in ice screws every few steps. Then he came to a halt and retreated, falling the last few feet. The problem seemed to be the impossible choice between two types of ice. On one side was a smooth cascade of melted and refrozen ice which was totally impervious to the axe whilst on the other was a sort of filigree brash which could take no weight at all.

This technical climbing was just the stuff I had avoided like the plague in the past but having penetrated so far I definitely felt a pang of regret that I hadn't improved my climbing skills over the previous years and thus widened our options. As it was, the pressure of time wouldn't have allowed us much leeway. The scale of operation the Chinese would have insisted on for a full attempt on Ulugh Mustagh from this side beggared the imagination. At least honour was satisfied – Tim had reached about half way and left it at that.

The first signs of a drop in morale came the next morning when the Chinese couldn't be bothered to heat breakfast whilst Tim and I demounted the tents. There was an ill-humoured, but mercifully short exchange of views and we had hot breakfasts for the rest of the expedition. The general irascibility continued, however.

"Tim notable by his absence during loading. He's half apathetic and half irritable at the moment," notes my diary. I was by now becoming accustomed to Tim's tendency to wander off, both mentally and physically, if unstimulated, although always with a certain absent-minded decorum, rather like a camel in a dinner jacket.

He meanwhile was describing me as "bad tempered" and "sharp". It was a passing disharmony – we were both feeling rather anticlimactic and the prospect of returning to full-time camel riding wasn't helping. Now the loads had reduced we were no longer sitting on a high platform above the baggage but instead astride the camel's back between the humps. It made shifting position much harder and put a heavy strain on the thighs. I didn't find it too bad but Tim had found it uncomfortable from the start and now worse every day.

The camels too were becoming desperate, bunching up and trying to eat the straw from the saddles. For the same reason we now had to remove and cover the saddles every evening. I found some dung in one of the holes in my saddle and fastidiously removed it, having to replace it when Hassim explained it was meant as a deterrent. Abdullah was obviously worried about his charges and our prospects looked bleak if they continued to die at the same rate as their predecessors. It was critical to get back to decent grazing as quickly as we could manage. Unfortunately this meant retracing our steps, itself a demoralising process and made worse by the contrast between our present condition and that of only a few weeks before. At least Abdullah showed no ill effects from recrossing the pass and his moustaches were erect once more. I wasn't sure whether the Diamox had helped his recovery but he obviously thought so and my prestige rose accordingly.

The first day we were to make a double march to Surveyors' Camp. We followed the same route as the approach to Camp 8, where we had a short halt and then climbed up the western slopes of the valley. The object was to cut the corner and avoid the valley terraces but we soon found ourselves crossing a succession of low transverse valleys. Dawn was constantly stumbling as though he had put his foot in a rodent hole and although he always recovered, it kept me on edge all day. For some obscure reason connected with camel psychology the bell had now been moved forward to the camel third from the rear, so we could easily have lost two camels without the bell falling silent – often the only warning the backmarkers had stopped. Luckily it never happened. Instead the first baggage camel pulled its noseplug out, spattering blood over its neighbours. Hassim rigged a jury halter. Only Seyn was as active as ever. She even caught one of the small rodents before it made it back to its hole.

Towards the north-north-east we could now see Rabbit Lake perched on the opposite shoulder of the valley. We had been too low to see it on the approach. Behind it, over fifty miles away, glinted the summits of Przhevalsky's Mosco range culminating in his Mount Kremlin.

We kept silently on all day, towards evening descending into a dusty amphitheatre and escaping through a narrow outlet into the main valley. We crossed the terraces to Surveyors Camp having covered twenty-five miles, the longest stage of the expedition.

We collected the remains of the bamboo poles and made a fire, feasting on cumin-flavoured kebabs. By now night had fallen and the temperature had plummeted. We crowded round the flames for warmth, whilst the camels wailed in the background. When the bamboo ran out we grubbed up roots from the stunted shrubs dotted around camp. So far we had tried to avoid destroying the already sparse vegetation but "needs must" and as the petrol ran low we made fires for cooking every night from now on.

We took no short cuts the next morning and spent the day crossing and recrossing the Ulugh Sou in the main valley. A lone ass stood on the valley side watching us pass. What on earth did it make of our strange caravan? Would it dream of us tonight?

As we plodded north the sun beat back from the flanking slopes and we shed our clothes layer by layer. By mid-afternoon the temperature had reached 77°F (24.8°C). Since it had fallen to 9°F (−13.1°C) the previous night, this marked our greatest daily range, 68°F (37°C). Dutreuil de Rhins had observed a similar variation whilst reconnoitring in the surrounding mountains. I later made a comparison of our temperatures and those of our predecessors for the US National Science Foundation. Hedin's proved to be about 9°F (5°C) higher on average although a month earlier in the year, but Dutreuil de Rhins' were between 4°F (2°C) and 36°F (20°C) lower for the same time of year. However hard our life seemed we were getting a comparatively easy ride. Unfortunately the number of positions was too small to come to wider conclusions about historical change.

In the late afternoon we came on the depot we had left on the approach and halted. Tim wanted to get a closer look at a herd of twenty wild yak about a mile away above a nearby terrace and set off for the brow just as I spied a lone yak grazing further down the river bed. I decided to stalk this as it was closer and the terraces and scrub provided some cover. I set off, getting within a hundred yards before he caught my scent and his head came up. From then on the best course of action seemed the tried and tested subtlety of walking straight for him with my camera poised. He was very large, very black and very shaggy but luckily I scared him more than he scared me and when I was about fifty yards away he broke, galloped to the terrace, climbed its slope at a trot and disappeared over the rim.

When I returned to the depot the loads were lying beside the camels and Huang was dancing up and down whilst screaming hysterically at the whole party. "It's happened – he's finally flipped," commented Tim disdainfully.

The main problem seemed to be that Abdullah and Hassim had simply loosed the loads without any discussion whilst Huang wanted to collect the depot and press on further. To compound this he was also worried about the "danger" posed by the yaks and he and Tim had already clashed about the risks of peeping over the terrace – the latest in a growing number of such exchanges as they had developed a mutual antipathy even stronger than that between Huang and myself.

I had assumed we were staying here and we certainly weren't going to reload the camels. Abdullah and Hassim had already started to unpack so we joined in. But as soon as George and the others moved to help Huang started up again, haranguing them whilst they stood, indecisive and sheepish amongst the waiting baggage. This continued whilst we carried the tents to the base of the terrace and started to mount them. The row slowly subsided as Abdullah lit a fire and started a brew but there was still no sign of action from the Chinese who by now were all sitting on their backsides and contemplating their navels. I asked George what was happening.

"Mr Huang wants to go on. He has forbidden us to unpack or to cook. Not all Chinese are like Huang. He will be dismissed in Urumqi. I am sorry. I am only small potato," was his unhappy reply.

The present little difficulty aside, Huang seemed determined to turn our already speedy retreat into a wholesale flight. Now we were headed for home his enthusiasm knew no bounds. But whilst the camels needed good pasture it was a fine gamble how fast they could be pushed to reach it and both the camels and Abdullah had their limits.

It seemed best to let Huang cool down so Tim and I carried on with the tents. After he had mounted the first of the geodesic tents I called him to help me with the Chinese tent, always the most difficult and made doubly so by the rising wind. By now the zip was totally shot and it was impossible to find a full set of usable pegs. Also the design was anything but stable. Five minutes later both of us were lying helpless with laughter as the tent collapsed on top of us for the third time. Then as we emerged a particularly strong gust loosed the geodesic tent from its temporary anchors and lifted it bodily into the air. Before we had time to grasp what had happened it was alternately bouncing and flying, fully erected, back towards Surveyor's Camp. Tim held on to the Chinese tent whilst I set off in hot pursuit.

At first I assumed it would ground and stick but every time I came near a new gust would lift it up and it would race off like an oversize kite catching the evening sun as it rose above the terrace.

After a couple of hundred yards I had to slow to a walk and George and Abdullah came up puffing beside me. It was nearly a mile before the tent stuck into a terrace and we could catch it. It was completely undamaged and we flew it back to camp helped by Da Wei who had followed. The episode could have been serious and certainly showed how our concentration was failing but in the circumstances it had lent the final touch of high farce to an already ridiculous situation.

On return to camp we appeared to be back to square one and George and Wang Hai tried to coax Da Wei into taking over from Huang. But Da Wei, no fool he, declined and the four of them pottered around camp studiously avoiding any useful activity. As there didn't seem to be any change in Huang's position by the time we had finished erecting the tents, I told George to inform him that unless the Chinese cooked a hot meal, we would demount their tents forthwith. I'm sure George was more tactful in the translation but it had the desired effect.

Tim and I lay on the brow of the terrace taking turns with the binoculars whilst the food was prepared. The yak had sauntered off heavily to the east by now and as we watched them disappear into a side valley our attention was caught by another movement on the upper slopes about two miles away. For ten minutes we debated if it could be a herd of Marco Polo's sheep, *Ovis ammon polii*. The animals in our sights were tall, agile beasts, but so were Ovis polii which could range up to nearly six foot long and five foot high with a five foot spread of horns. And from time to time as they clambered upwards in groups of two or three we saw a flash of light beside the head, as though of horns catching the setting sun. But given the poor light and the distance we eventually had to admit the herd was just too indistinct to be sure and could just as easily be antelope or even kyang.

There were plenty of antelope and kyang about the next day – and a hawk circling high over the caravan for much of the morning. We passed Camp Six after an hour and Camp Five a couple of hours later, continuing north towards the three river confluence and into new country.

Moving to the eastern edge of the valley we soon after passed under a rocky cliff where the camel bell echoed back to make a doleful peal which spooked the camels. By now the river had disappeared into the sand and the terraces had flattened to a wide plain. The air seemed strangely oppressive and then came an insidious hissing which grew as a curtain of dust filled the northern horizon. In minutes it was upon us and we were enveloped in a sea of sand. My eyes, nose and mouth filled with fine grit however tightly I tried to pull my cowl and we progressed as ghosts hardly able to see each other in the gathering murk. It continued like this for half an hour then as quickly as it had started it ceased and, looking back, we could see it rolling up the valley behind us.

An hour later we entered a band of crescent dunes – each dune standing isolated on the flat valley floor oblivious of its neighbours. We passed silently between them. The sun, absent until now, appeared low in the west, casting rhythmic shadows on the sensuous slopes.

Towards dusk we entered a marshy area and threaded between salt-rimmed pools to camp on solid ground beneath an isolated hill. The site was a few miles to the west of the supposed river confluence and the crystal clear stream which left the marsh to skirt our camp was a minor mystery. It could have been the resurgent Ulugh Sou, a minor tributary of the Toghru Sou, or even the Toghru Sou itself. Identification was difficult as Abdullah gave the name "Toghru Sou" indiscriminately to the individual river and the whole area. This was typical of our problem. For in such unfrequented regions few features merited individual names. "Musluk", for instance, was applied to any peak in the extensive mountain range we were about to cross, a river (which didn't pass through the range) and several passes (which did).

When researching I had been sent up many a blind alley by variations on the same theme. One explorer after another had

come back with maps covered in contradictory names supplied
by his camel men. Both the Altyn Tagh and the Chimen Tagh
had moved from the south to the north of the Valley of the Winds
and back again over the decades (the Chimen Tagh are now to
the south, the Altyn Tagh to the north). To confuse matters
further the Altyn Tagh were (and still are) often confused with
the Arka Tagh. The supposedly definitive biography of Hedin by
American academic George Kish makes this elementary mistake.
The Arka Tagh for variation merely shuffled east then west (although I notice a recent tendency to the east again).

Even when features were fixed there was no guarantee that the
name would be easily identifiable, Bash Malghun, Tura, Bash
Malakung, Tula, Bash Molga, Bach Malghoun and Pa Shi Ma
Erh Kung being a single prime example. The problem continues
today with the attempted replacement of local names by Beijing
government substitutes and the uncritical reproduction of these
in such prestigious publications as the Royal Geographical
Society's *Mountains of Central Asia.*

Emerging from the tent the next morning I caught my last
brief glimpse of Ulugh Mustagh, its shining peaks dimly outlined
in the southern sky. We had covered the intervening sixty miles
in only three days and the camels wouldn't survive if we kept up
this pace. Our fodder was almost exhausted and Abdullah was
desperate to take advantage of the comparative luxuriance
around us. Two months before I would have regarded this spot
as hard and desolate but lazing now beside the babbling brook
with the indulgence of one or two scattered plants in sight it
seemed indescribably fertile. At last I could see how Abdullah
could describe these few scattered clumps of orange-yellow grass
as "lush grazing". We agreed to stay an extra day and the camels
were loosed to plunge into an orgy of mastication before we faced
the Musluk Tagh.

We spent most of the morning trying to open Tim's camera as
the winder, which also acted as latch, had fallen by the wayside.
I felt a residual responsibility for the good behaviour of the

machine as I had sold it to Tim just before leaving England. More subtle methods having failed we eventually jemmied it open watched by a disapproving nuthatch perched on the tent.

In the afternoon we crowded into one of the tents to discuss our return route – all except Wang Hai and George who couldn't fit and poked their heads in through the tentflap. This was the most acrimonious discussion of the whole expedition and brought our differences to a head. Huang was determined to press on as fast as possible to Bash Malghun and proposed taking the route over the Gold Washers' Pass. In contrast Tim and I, having compromised on the return route so far were determined to take this last opportunity to descend the Charchan Gorge originally proposed by Huang for the approach. Huang said we didn't have government permission for the route but how he reconciled this with our earlier discussions was beyond us. Try as we would, we never could understand how he could seriously trot out such transparent lies and defend them for hours at a time. The negotiations before the expedition had been wearing enough but it had been even more depressing to find them continuing throughout its prosecution. It was as if Huang had packed his Academy desk when he set out.

I didn't imagine he was being purposely obstructive but simply out of his depth, his attitude swinging wildly between bombast and supplication. I recognised he had been under constant pressure from Abdullah, as now, to take the easiest route for the camels and had even shown occasional flashes of friendliness but my overwhelming feeling was one of anger that our otherwise exhilarating journey had been marred by such unnecessary haggling.

For his part Huang complained that I was arrogant and had outdated imperialist attitudes. My impatience with the confusion and deceit no doubt did have similarities with that of my predecessors but it was this same confusion and deceit which had made it impossible to build up mutual respect and trust. For the time being I turned Huang's argument on its head and insisted we descend the first half of the gorge and cut over the Musluk Pass used by Pevtsov – as we had agreed in Urumqi. How would his superiors take his refusal to follow the approved route?

Two hours later the discussion was going nowhere and Da Wei announced he wanted to make a contribution – for the first time on the expedition.

"Oh good, we might hear some sense at last," exclaimed Tim.

Having longer experience of Chinese bureaucracy I suspected he would be disappointed. And so he was – Da Wei repeating all Huang's points and concluding with;

"Let us maintain the friendship between our Two Great Peoples. If there are contradictions in our positions we must discuss them. Let us make a start."

Tim's eyes glazed over, the meeting eventually breaking up with the matter unresolved. At the end of it all I couldn't help suspecting that Huang was just a little scared of the gorge. We were both mad but Tim was livid and wanted the two of us to simply leave on foot down the gorge. It's my second great regret that I talked him out of it.

We went instead for an evening walk over the plain to cool down. Towards dusk a large herd of Orongo antelope came sweeping round the corner of the eastern mountains and halted to graze near the river confluence. We stalked them to within a quarter of a mile before they ran off to the south, a rearguard with majestic horns protecting their retreat.

The sight of such imposing animals in the wild couldn't fail to revive our spirits and they were raised further when, later that night Tim and I took turns to scan the night sky with the binoculars. The whole canopy stretched above us as clearly as could be, its black depths filled with an ocean of stars. Lying on my back on the frozen ground and looking upward I could almost feel the earth pilot its way between them. As I watched a shooting star erupted across the steady track of a satellite and I was left to contrast the powerful beauty of the greater order around us with the sordid indignity of the day's discussions.

CHAPTER 11

Via Dolorosa

The whole camp was in a foul mood the next morning. In addition to the unresolved tensions over the route, Hassim was limping and terrorising every camel in reach. It came as no great surprise to find he had been badly kicked whilst collecting the herd together. He couched them with a firm "Tushabje" which I assumed was somewhat stronger than the usual "Chuga".

An hour after starting we passed a mudstone monolith about ten feet high covered in the etched graffiti of itinerant gold miners. Then we entered the gorge of the Charchan Darya, its gates guarded on the north by an isolated outlier rising above lower screes to a craggy summit. Here the listless stream of the Toghru Sou was charged by the milky waters of the more vigorous Musluk Sou. Of the Ulugh Sou there was no sign and I could only assume it had evaporated completely or percolated through the marshes around our camp.

Once past the outlier we watched Abdullah carefully to see which way he would swing. On our left on the far side of the river was a gigantic scree ramp leading up to the Gold Washers Pass, Littledale's route. Ahead the Charchan Darya led down a wide gorge flanked by rocky walls. Above, from time to time, we could see the snow-plastered slopes of the surrounding peaks. The tension was terrific as Abdullah held on down the gorge. Had Huang misread the map, was he simply a good guy striving to please or had our implied threats worked? We will never know but the result was we left the Gold Washers Pass behind.

The valley floor continued wide, the river gradually gaining in momentum and swirling from side to side. We climbed with difficulty on to the sloping terraces on the right bank, here composed of camel-foot-sized boulders and very unpopular with our mounts. Keeping in close below the right-hand cliffs as the gorge swept first left then right around the interlocking spurs we alternately climbed and descended the flanking scree.

There were several tributaries feeding into the gorge, mostly on the left bank, but, bizarrely, these hung suspended above the main valley floor, their cross sections cut through where the Charchan Darya had scoured into the scree. It was strange how frost and floodwater had conspired to create features not unlike the hanging valleys seen in glaciated areas.

After two hours' difficult progress we came across the remains of several recent gold washers' camps, the fireplaces and circular outlines of their former tents being clearly visible. At one camp there was a succession of holes and races in a form of sluice. The system, known as Placer mining, was the same as that described by Hedin and others and entailed nothing more than digging out the surface deposits and washing them to reveal minute particles of the sought-after metal.

According to Hedin the gold washers' season lasted only two months during which they laboured unremittingly, living on flat bread and any meat the accompanying hunters could shoot. Yet by all accounts it appears to have been a desperate gamble. Grenard describes meeting a party of gold washers returning to Charchan.

> The poor fellows had reaped more misery than gold; and the same men whom I had seen a few months before on the road from Nia to Cherchen, full of spirits and gaiety in the rain and hail, I now saw hanging their heads, dragging their feet, shivering as they held the pitiful rags of their clothes to their emaciated bodies, while the sun shone in vain to warm them, for they had nothing left in their wallets, not even hope.

The most productive sites seem to have been further east, the best known being at Bokalyk on the far side of the Achik Kol Plain. Graham Sandberg, an early twentieth century writer on Tibet, even suggested that these mines had been visited by Guillaume Boucher, a Parisian goldsmith resident in Karakorum in

1254. Boucher would thus have predated Przhevalsky's sighting of the Arka Tagh by a good six centuries, but as Sandberg misplaced Karakorum itself by over a thousand miles, his speculation on Boucher's travels has to be taken with a large pinch of salt.

Przhevalsky too came across the mines, commenting;

> Gold is everywhere abundant, and will be the first bait to tempt hither the avaricious European.

Yet contrary to his prediction, mining appears to have fallen into disuse over the following century, reviving only recently in an unofficial and probably illegal fashion. No doubt it will soon tempt others from further afield but I suspect avaricious plundering of the natural reserves of Tibet and Xinjiang will not, this time, come from the west.

The gorge slowly narrowed, eventually closing completely on the river. We were faced with climbing over the right-hand spur along the vestiges of a track cut into the hillside. Abdullah and Hassim led the camels in single file ahead whilst the rest of us followed behind. The day's grazing at Toghru Sou had had little effect and the camels were still exhausted, stumbling and rearing as the edge of the track crumbled into the river below. At two particularly steep sections they stopped completely until urged gently on – this was no place for severe discipline.

There was a dry-stone cairn on top of the spur and from here we could look down the next section of the gorge. It opened out once again and in a growing swathe of sunshine the sandy slopes, white-edged water and blue sky looked almost welcoming. Progress was certainly easier as we crossed and recrossed the relatively docile river. Only when the bed dipped again did we have to return upstream to find a safe crossing to the left bank. Here a rough stone wall had been built against the base of an overhanging cliff. At first I thought it was a shelter but there was no door and Abdullah said it was a tomb for one of the gold washers who hadn't made it back to Charchan.

Just after the cliff Abdullah turned left towards the Musluk

Pass. This was the route Pevtsov had taken in 1890. The main gorge continued straight on then dipped and turned right, disappearing between rocky cliffs towards the east. It was tempting to simply pull aside and follow this but the Musluk Pass was an implicit compromise.

The lower valley leading up to the pass was narrower than usual and filled with old landslips which made progress slow and tortuous. Later it widened and we zigzagged our way slowly upwards. The peaks on either side shone in the late afternoon sun then disappeared as the valley steepened and narrowed again. Eventually we were climbing up a dark rock-strewn funnel. By now our camels were blowing hard, even Huang had dismounted and the party had become strung out over a quarter of a mile. At intervals we crushed piles of white sticks underfoot, then coming on the first of many skulls I realised we were walking on the skeletons of dead camels. The pass was littered with bones in every stage of decay. But we were not yet done – as the funnel steepened further a human skull poked from a rough grave at the side of the route. A last push and the funnel opened out. Seyn had rushed ahead and now stood stiff and proud as one by one the camels and humans dragged themselves on to the grey summit of the pass.

Behind the funnel disappeared into the depths of the Charchan Darya gorge, its gloom contrasting all the more strongly with the golden peaks beyond. Ahead the pass hung above a wider valley falling hazily to the west.

We started down after a short break. The valley floor was filled with a labyrinth of small ravines cut into the all-pervasive scree and having taken slightly different lines we soon became separated. There was little real danger of losing each other as the general trend was westward. When my ravine veered to the north I climbed the flanking slope and bumped into Tim. We followed the ridge which was higher than the surrounding country, but still within the main valley, and sat for a while watching our colleagues thresh around in the maze below.

Later we all met at the western edge of the ravines. Everyone was tired and it was time to camp, but predictably the valley was still dry. We pressed on hoping for water, encouraged by the occasional but deceptive patch of scraggy grazing. Dusk was already falling and we were giving up hope when we came on a slow moving stream and, on the earth terrace above, the remains of a deserted camp. It had been our longest day, ten hours, and we had covered a more than respectable twenty-four miles, including the five mile climb up to the pass.

Tim and I cooked the last of the dehydrated rations in the hearth of one of the yurt bases whilst George and the others fought with the tents. After eating we sorted through the discarded ration packs in the forlorn hope of finding more cheese. Whilst preparing in England we, or rather our girlfriends, had thrown most "inessentials" such as cheese and boiled sweets out of the packs leaving only dried meals and desserts. Unfortunately in practice we couldn't be bothered with the desserts and, no doubt due to some great metabolic yearning, were desperate to get our hands on cheese and sweets. Luckily the Chinese had brought some sweets from Urumqi, so we were satisfied on that score but only a few plastic sausages of processed smoked cheese had slipped through the censorship process and these were at a premium. For a while I had lived in hopes that the Chinese, who normally hate cheese, would refuse their share, but they had chosen this moment to discover a new-found affection for it and Tim and I were now reduced to splitting our last portion. There was a distinct tension in the air as the knife went in. Every mouthful was delicious and I shall look upon processed cheese in a much more benign light in future.

We woke the next morning to find ourselves at the junction of two valleys dominated on the north by a sunlit snow-capped massif. These were probably the highest peaks in the Musluk Tagh but Abdullah had no separate name for them. To say the scene was almost Alpine would be to ignore the continuing aridity and dustiness of the landscape, but it was certainly much

less alien and sterile than our recent surroundings. The camp
was used by shepherds from Bash Malghun who brought their
flocks up for the summer grazing and it had only recently been
vacated. Small caches of cooking utensils had been left in the
fireplaces when camp had been struck and, as a token, we left
some of our own pots behind. Besides the yurt bases and fireplaces there was an underground cave with a wooden door and
several makeshift sleeping hollows cut into the soft earth cliff
above the stream. There was also a fair sized pit about five feet
deep on the flat part of the site. This, explained Abdullah, was
used as a stock enclosure.

Possibly in celebration of nearing home Abdullah made the
first brew of the day with lashings of milk and sugar, very much
to my taste – unlike the alternative with milk and salt – and we
set off refreshed down the valley to the west.

When the valley sides closed in again we found ourselves
climbing a rough track cut into the rock face high above the
stream, this time complicated by an unavoidable rock which projected at saddle height just as the summit was turned. But it
passed without incident and we made good progress on the
downward leg.

Early in the afternoon we were confronted by a sheer wall of
mountains barring the end of the valley. Bash Malghun lay only
ten miles away on the far side of that wall but it stretched unbroken across our route and we would have to circumnavigate its
western end before we could regain the Valley of the Winds.

We turned left in front of the wall and spent the rest of the day
climbing and descending a series of deep terraces in the valley
bottom. There was a strong smell of thyme in one valley, although I couldn't find the source and later we entered a band of
low bell heather-like shrubs.

Towards the end of the afternoon Hassim pointed out a dust
cloud travelling parallel to us on the far side of the valley. This
grew until we could first see the cause, a flock of sheep, and later
pick out two donkeys following behind. It was half an hour before

our paths finally converged, though having once pointed out the dust cloud Hassim studiously ignored it and even when the shepherd came up with us his greeting was determinedly offhand. The rest of us exchanged similar nods of welcome to the first new face we had seen since leaving Bash Malghun.

The white-bearded shepherd was accompanied by his daughter, or possibly granddaughter, a small girl who kept out of the way of the foreigners and Chinese and busied herself chasing runaways with a long stick. She wore a dusty cotton jacket and trousers and sandwiched between them, in heart raising anarchy, a gold brocade dress.

We travelled together until the valley widened out and set up our last camp, Camp 16, in a loop of the stream surrounded by green scrub. We had covered twenty-two miles in six and a half hours, our fastest day at nearly three and a half miles an hour. It was a strange paradox that our exhausted and shrunken camels were now travelling faster than ever before. Obviously the lack of heavy loads was a major factor and the lower altitude a second but I also suspected the camels knew they were nearing home. And Abdullah and Hassim's firm and occasionally bad-tempered encouragement shouldn't be discounted. The drawback was that our camels, unlike horses, became more uncomfortable the faster they travelled and we had spent much of the day riding the swell on a very choppy sea.

That night we gathered round the camp fire for the last time and finished the remains of the lamb. It had lasted well in the rarefied air of the mountains but was almost a month old by now and fairly high. Even so, well grilled and covered in cumin it was still in demand. Seyn too gorged herself on the discarded carcass.

We sat and talked late into the night, all acrimony temporarily forgotten, our bearded faces and bloody lips grotesque in the flickering firelight. Then I rose and to the accompaniment of the crackling fire and murmuring conversation took my last skyward panorama of endless space and mountain silhouette.

CHAPTER 12

Postscript

Our return to Bash Malghun the next day was in the same minor key as our meeting with the shepherd, the population being fully occupied with their newly returned flocks. Seyn ran ahead to announce our arrival but only a few children ran out to greet us and not until the camels were finally couched did a noisy crowd gather to help and quiz Abdullah and Hassim on their adventure. We dismounted for the last time, rather more confidently than we had first mounted a month before. By my reckoning we had completed 316 miles at an average of 16 miles a day, excluding rest days.

Our first indulgence on arrival was a wash, Tim and I stripping and sharing a bucket of lukewarm water. In my case it obviously had a limited effect, Tim's diary describing my appearance as "diabolical" even after the wash. The rest of the day was spent dispersing the caravan so laboriously collected. Wang Da Wei revealed an unopened case of tinned meat he had carefully nurtured through the expedition and Huang promptly sold it. Later Tim and I took Abdullah and Hassim aside to formally thank them and give them our hardly baptised climbing rope. We also bought some of the cloth we had seen woven, a transaction which necessitated a whole string of middlemen including George. Unlike the others he didn't take a cut while we were present, but he later had to go back for something he had forgotten.

That night we were invited to Abdullah's house for a *tamasha*. He may have been poor but his house was one of the most pleasant, with a walled courtyard to the front containing the village's largest tree. In the absence of Arak the gathering was considerably more restrained than our send-off party but it obviously put the seal on his new standing in the community. We sat together with his friends and relatives on the raised platform which acted as both bed and lounge and made small-talk whilst eating succulent young lamb, the antithesis of the previous night's strong fare. We were served by Abdullah's children and were told his wife was still with their flock in the mountains.

We made a sad departure the next morning and were soon to be found in the familiar huddle around a dead jeep. After pushing, pulling and towing for an hour we eventually left it and transferred to the accompanying truck, arriving in Charchan in the middle of the night perched on top of two tons of stone and accompanied by six terrified sheep.

It is best to draw a veil over our stay in Charchan, which had a frustrating similarity to the earlier wait in Urumqi, but this time garnished with an all-pervasive diarrhoea. Jean Paul Sartre, not a particularly cheery author at the best of times, becomes almost hallucinatory when you have spent a day with him perched over an earth privy in Charchan.

We eventually flew out to Urumqi via Korla on 5th October. The following day we were feted at a "Victory" banquet with the Branch President of the Academy, Teng Tingkang, and parted from most of our colleagues with genuine regret and affection. Wang Hai in particular was very emotional and gave us small presents from his children. But it was too good to last. We were informed that a further four camels had died and ended the expedition as we had begun, haggling over expenses late into the night.

We bade farewell to Huang at the airport early the next morning. In the mountains I could have happily strangled him but already the mellowing process of hindsight had set in and I almost felt sorry for him. Bureaucratic and untrained for initiative, Huang was simply an extreme example of the culture in which he thrived. This had been amply illustrated when his superiors had attributed our problems to the lack of a radio – "We would have been able to relay orders to Mr Huang from

Urumqi."

Whatever I thought of Huang, the prospect of carrying on a remote three-way exchange with Urumqi sounded infinitely worse. In a way I had been foolish to think it would be otherwise, for our problems had been amply rehearsed on previous joint expeditions.

On the plane we took stock. Tim had withstood being a tool of my ambition with admirable fortitude and even admitted to having enjoyed the odd moment. For my part I was content to have completed my ten-year journey at last. The expedition had been very different to my vague imaginings of a decade before but it had proved no less exhilarating for all that.

I still regretted we hadn't pushed up more but we had done the best we could. Our eight man, nineteen camel and one dog party had, after all, been relatively modest compared to the travelling towns of both Littledale and modern Himalayan expeditions, and the logistical problems of travelling in such remote areas still seem to constrain any sustained effort at the furthest extent.

But for those with the stamina and tenacity to match their dreams, the Arka Tagh and the surrounding ranges of the Kun Lun are one of the last strongholds of adventure. There in the measureless distance of Asia's mountains and deserts you will still find unknown lakes and unclimbed passes – and enduring wonder in the power and mystery of nature's wild extremities.

Bibliography

Ambolt, Nils – *Karavan,* London 1939.

Bates, Robert H. – *The Ulugh Muztagh,* In The American Alpine Journal, New York, Vol 28 1986. pp 27-38.

Bonvalot, Gabriel – *De Paris au Tonking à travers le Tibet inconnu,* Paris 1891. Translated as *Across Tibet,* London 1891.

Bruce, Clarence Dalrymple – *In the Footsteps of Marco Polo,* London 1907.

Chen, Jack – *The Sinkiang Story,* London 1977.

Dabbs, Jack A. – *History of the Discovery and Exploration of Chinese Turkestan,* The Hague 1963.

Danziger, Nick – *Danziger's Travels,* London 1987.

Fleming, Peter – *News from Tartary,* London 1936.

Galwan, Ghulam Rassul – *Servant of Sahibs,* Cambridge 1923.

Grenard, Fernand and Dutreuil de Rhins, Jules – *Mission Scientifique dans la Haute Asie 1890-95,* Paris 1897-8. Abridged and translated as *Tibet, the Country and its Inhabitants,* London 1904.

Hart-Davis, Duff – *Peter Fleming,* London 1974.

Haslund, Henning – *Men and Gods in Mongolia,* London 1935.

Hedin, Sven – *Through Asia,* London 1898. *Central Asia and Tibet,* London 1903. *Scientific Results of a Journey in Central Asia 1899-1902,* Stockholm 1904-7. *My Life As An Explorer,* London 1926.

Hopkirk, Peter – *Foreign Devils on the Silk Road,* London 1980. *Trespassers on the Roof of the World,* London 1982.

Huxley, A. (Editor) – *Standard Encyclopaedia of the World's Mountains,* London 1962.

Kish, George – *To the Heart of Asia,* Ann Arbor 1984.

Lias, Godfrey – *Kazak Exodus*, London 1956.

Littledale, St George – *A Journey Across Tibet From North to South, And West To Ladak*, In Geographical Journal, London, Vol 7 1896, pp 453-478 and map p 576. Obituary (by Sir Francis Younghusband) In Geographical Journal, London, Vol 78 1931, pp 95-6.

Maillart, Ella K. – *Forbidden Journey*, London 1937.

Molnar, Peter – *Ulugh Muztagh: The Highest Peak on the North Tibetan Plateau*, In the Alpine Journal, London, Vol 92 1987, pp 104-116. *Direct Measurements of the Height of Ulugh Muztagh, Reputedly the Highest Peak in the Kunlun, Northern Tibet*, (with others) In EOS Washington DC 1986 pp 1337-9. *Geologic Evolution of Northern Tibet: Results of an Expedition to Ulugh Muztagh* (with others) In Science, USA, Vol 235 1987, pp 299-305.

Morgan, E. Delmar – *Journey of Carey and Dalgleish in Chinese Turkestan and Northern Tibet (Mr Dalgleish's Itinerary);* and *General Prejevalsky on the Orography of Northern Tibet*, In RGS Supplementary Papers, London Vol 3 1893, pp 1-86.

Pevtsov, M. V. – *Trudy Tibetskoy ekspeditsii, 1889-90*, St Petersburg 1892-6.

Pilkington, John – *An Adventure on the Old Silk Road*, London 1989.

Polo, Marco – *The Travels*, Penguin edition translated and edited by Ronald Latham, London 1958.

Przhevalsky, Nikolai – *Ot Kyakhty na istoki Zholtoy reki*, St Petersburg 1888 Chapter 7 translated in RGS Supplementary Papers, London, Vol 3 1893 pp 57-86.

Rayfield, Donald – *The Dream of Lhasa*, London 1976.

Royal Geographical Society – *The Mountains of Central Asia*, London 1987.

Sandberg, Samuel Louis Graham – *The Exploration of Tibet: Its History and Particulars 1623-1904*, Calcutta 1904.

Schomberg, R. C. F. – *Peaks and Plains of Central Asia*, London 1933.

Stein, Sir Mark Aurel – *On Ancient Central Asian Tracks*, London 1933.
Wellby, M. S. – *Through Unknown Tibet*, London 1898.
Zhang, Mingtao – *The Roof of the World*, Beijing 1982.

Additional Maps

Atlas of False Colour Landsat Images of China. Science Press, Beijing 1983. Scale 1:500,000.
Landsat MSS Satellite Images. Nos. 152 34, 21.12.76; 152 35, 21.12.76; 153 34, 16.11.76.
Operational Navigation Charts. US Defense Mapping Agency. Nos. G7 and G8. Scale 1:1,000,000.
Petermanns Geographische Mitteilungen 1899-1900. In RGS Map Room Refs. S321 and S322. Scale 1:1,000,000.
Surveys and Explorations – Himalaya and Central Asia: Survey of India 1934. In RGS Map Room Ref. Asia Div. 21. Scale 1:8,000,000.

Note: At the time of writing I believe Nick and Betsy Clinch are preparing the Littledales' diaries for publication and Jim Perrin is writing a biography of Eric Shipton.

Index